National Trust Recipes

For Janet
    Best wishes
Sarah Edington

Cookery books published by the National Trust

Healthy Eating by Sarah Edington

Teatime Recipes by Jane Pettigrew

Picnics by Kate Crookenden, Margaret Willes and Caroline Worlledge

Celebrations: Recipes for Festive Occasions by Simone Sekers

The Art of Dining by Sara Paston-Williams

A Book of Historical Recipes by Sara Paston-Williams

National Trust Recipes

Sarah Edington

THE NATIONAL TRUST

To John, Eliza and Jesse

First edition published 1988
Second, completely revised, edition published 1996
by National Trust (Enterprises) Ltd
36 Queen Anne's Gate
London SW1H 9AS

ISBN 0 7078 0251 2

British Library Cataloguing-in-Publication Data.
A catalogue record of this book is available from the British Library.

Illustrations by Catherine Broom-Lynne, Brian Delf, John Finnie,
Claude Page, Eric Thomas, Soun Vannithone

Designed by Newton Engert Partnership

Phototypeset in Monotype Sabon Series 669
by Southern Positives and Negatives (SPAN), Lingfield, Surrey

Printed in England
by BAS Printers Limited, Over Wallop, Hampshire

The National Trust is an independent
registered charity (number 205846)

CONTENTS

Acknowledgements

The author and publishers would like to thank the following for so generously providing recipes and advice for this book.

Baddesley Clinton – Richard Newall, Barbara Freeman

Biddulph Grange Garden – Anne Wilde, Lynda Moss

Buckland Abbey – Jane Wood, Elizabeth Ingram, Steve Cornforth,
   Sally Whitfield, Amy Harris

Calke Abbey – Helen Jerome, Emma Carlier

Cliveden – Julie Cullen, Jo Smith

Erddig – Pat Bodymore, Ellen Jeffries, Nia Jones

Flatford Mill – Jan Burtles, Catherine Cole

Florence Court – Kathleen Ellaott, Linda Pagett

Fountains Abbey – Sharon Wilkinson, Grace Elford

The Giant's Causeway – Adrian Fletcher, Maire Murphy

Ham House – Gill Sims, Debbie Potter

Kedleston Hall – Anne Parkin

Killerton – Dorothy Martin, David Pike, Christine Hewitt

Lanhydrock – Angela Coombs, Jackie Kamkiew, Tracy Stanlake

Montacute – Shirley Santos

Mount Stewart – Margaret Dorrian

Oxburgh Hall – Alison Sloane

Powis Castle – Diane Henry, Elspeth Humphreys

St Michael's Mount – Jayne Spenceley, Michelle Webb, Joy Nankervis

Saltram – Pauline Gill

Souter Lighthouse – Lyn Bayse

Standen – Barbara Twiss

Stowe Landscape Garden – Carol Cook

Sutton House – Glen Sillett, Justin P. Derrick, Maureen McKenzie

Trerice – Mary Parsons

Wallington – Frances Johnson, Sue Reed

Watersmeet – Jackie Prideaux

York Tea-Room – Anne Chamberlain
   and Sue Wright, the National Trust's Catering Manager

INTRODUCTION

Nine years ago I travelled all over England and Wales visiting the remarkably varied properties of the National Trust, talking to the cooks who provide the good food in the restaurants and tea-rooms. The result was *The Book of National Trust Recipes*: a collection of delicious recipes, some traditional, some innovative, some simple, some more elaborate, but all rewarding to cook and good to eat.

It has been a great pleasure to set off on my travels again, this time adding Northern Ireland to my itinerary. I made some delightful discoveries: as well as magnificent castles, houses and gardens, I was fascinated to find that a lighthouse at Souter in Tyne and Wear and the extraordinary Giant's Causeway in Antrim were also in the care of the Trust. The greatest discovery though, was that the good British cooking I found nine years ago still flourishes. Not only that, the enthusiasm and enterprise of the cooks enabled me to produce an entirely new collection of recipes. Only the recipe for egg custard features in both books.

All the strengths of the Trust's restaurants appear in the recipes. Interesting, sustaining soups such as Red Pepper, Butter-bean and Ham, Pea, Pear and Watercress, are interspersed with main courses for light or hearty appetites. How about Welsh Lamb and Leek Casserole, Beef and Vegetable Pottage served with Norfolk Dumpling, or Bulgur Shepherd's Pie – a tasty vegetarian version of an old favourite?

Some recipes reflect the clientele of the restaurant. Those from Sutton House in East London have Afro-Caribbean and Asian origins, reflecting the multi-national community that surrounds the Tudor house. Vegetarian Lasagne from Waters-meet, an outstandingly beautiful valley of good strenuous walks in North Devon, will satisfy the most footsore rambler.

Puddings, cakes and biscuits, always a treat at a Trust restaurant, are well represented. You will find rich delights in the puddings hot and cold: indulge yourself with Chocolate Fudge Pudding, try the subtle Lemon Geranium Syllabub.

As I travelled round, I did notice two particular concerns. The first is an awareness of the importance and value of regional cooking and the need to cook, serve and write down the recipes if they are to survive. This awareness is reflected in the recipes, particularly for cakes, scones and teabreads. Bara Brith, a teabread from Wales, and the delightfully named Singin' Hinnies from Northumberland come to mind, but there are many more to choose from. The second is an increasing interest in historic food. Several recipes are adaptations of medieval, Tudor and Georgian recipes served at the restaurants as part of special historic menus. Do try them; the combination of fruit, vegetables, fish and meat sometimes seem odd but they do taste remarkably good.

Since these are mostly family recipes, quantities are also family size and will serve four to six people according to appetite. Where cakes are concerned, I have given a tin size. Some of the soups were difficult to reduce to one-meal quantities and you may well find that they will feed a further set of hungry mouths at another meal on the next day – alternatively, soup freezes very well. Eggs are all standard size 3 unless otherwise indicated. If no sugar variety is given, use caster sugar.

I have given cooking times and temperatures but please, please use them as an indication not an order. I have found from personal experience that every oven varies. Where cakes and sponge puddings are concerned, for instance, the best test is to plunge a stainless steel skewer into the centre of the cake or pudding – if it comes out clean, the cake or pudding is cooked. Most cakes should be taken out of their tins and cooled on a wire tray after cooking and only stored when they are cold. Similarly all biscuits should be cooled on a wire tray and put in a tin once they are cold. When re-heating dishes, be sure to heat them right through until they are bubbling and too hot to eat straightaway.

A word on measures. It is a knotty problem. As I write this, shops and super-markets have just been ordered to mark weights in kilos and grams, liquids are sold in litres and pints, and both imperial and metric weights for scales are still available in the shops. Full metrication is still several years away. After much soul searching I decided that the imperial measures should be listed first and metric second, but they are both given equal importance. You may have to buy in metric, in which case the amount you need is very easy to find, but I feel most people using this book will still be working with imperial weights. I have not provided metric equivalent for tea- and tablespoons as they are really too fiddly.

Finally can I draw your attention to one recipe that is entirely up to date? The Centenary Celebration Cake recipe from Oxburgh Hall in Norfolk tastes splendidly traditional but was invented in 1995 from scratch to celebrate the first 100 years of the National Trust. Taste, colour, texture, cost, time to make and time to bake, were all considered when it was planned. Above all it had to be 'special'. I think it was this last indefinable quality I was looking for on my travels and I hope you will agree with me that many of these recipes have it.

BADDESLEY CLINTON
WARWICKSHIRE

Baddesley Clinton is a small moated manor in the Forest of Arden. Today, what's left of the forest is peaceful parkland just south of the urban sprawl of Birmingham. Despite its modest size Baddesley Clinton has had a turbulent, sometimes violent, history which reflects the difficulties of the staunchly Catholic Ferrers family, its owners from 1517 until the Trust acquired it in 1980. Three centuries ago Catholics could find fellow believers here, hear the Mass said, and hide from religious persecution. Now it is a haven from those modern secular scourges of stress and noise.

This little manor has also been home to some far from modest characters whose outsize personalities live on in the windows and stones of the old house and the furniture, pictures and possessions visitors can still enjoy. Perhaps the first was Henry 'Antiquary' Ferrers who was squire for seventy years from 1564 until 1633.

He built the Great Parlour and started the glowing sequence of armorial glass now in the Great Hall and the Drawing Room. He was also a great trencherman. On 2 November 1622 he wrote in his diary: '... had to diner a necke of motton and potage, a piece of powdered biefe and cabage, a leg of goose broyled, a rabbet a piece of apple tart, cheese apples and pears ...'. He also recorded the indigestion that followed.

It is impossible not to be aware of Rebecca Dulcibella Orpen, her husband Marmion Ferrers (the last Ferrers to be squire of Baddesley Clinton), her uncle Edward Dering and her formidable aunt Lady Chatterton. Resident at Baddesley from 1867, they revelled in its history. They reinstated the ghost in the room where you can still see an indelible blood stain. (This, Henry Ferrers claimed, was where his ancestor Nicholas Brome had murdered a priest whom he discovered 'chockinge his wife under ye chinne'). They restored the chapel. They dressed up in seventeenth-century clothes and Rebecca Dulcibella recorded everything in pictures, still hanging on the walls, which bring their idealisation of the past vividly alive.

Four centuries after Antiquary Ferrers you still eat well in the Great Barn at Baddesley Clinton. Good local ingredients are turned into simple but none the less inventive recipes, including a soup using the fine early crop of nettles found in the hedgerows.

Butter-bean and Ham Soup

8 oz/225 g butter-beans
1 oz/25 g butter
1 onion, peeled and sliced
1 carrot, peeled and chopped
2 pints/1250 ml stock (ham
   stock is best, but use
   vegetarian stock cubes if it is
   not available)

GARNISH
2 oz/50 g diced ham
1 tablespoon parsley, chopped

Soak the butter-beans overnight. In a saucepan large enough to take all the ingredients, melt the butter, gently fry the onion and carrot for 5 minutes. Add the butter-beans and the stock. Bring to the boil, then simmer until the butter-beans are cooked, which will take up to an hour. Take off the heat, liquidise the mixture, and adjust the seasoning if you wish. Add the chopped ham and the parsley and serve piping hot.

Nettle and Watercress Soup

6oz/175g nettle tops
1oz/25g butter
1 medium onion, finely chopped
1¾ pints/1 litre vegetable stock
1 bunch of watercress
½ pint/250ml creamy milk
Pinch of chilli pepper
Salt and pepper to taste

GARNISH (optional)
Single cream and paprika

Pick only young, tender nettle leaves and wash well. Cook over a low heat just in the water they hold on their leaves until they are tender. Drain in a colander. Melt the butter in a large saucepan over a low heat. Add the onion and cook gently until it is cooked but not brown. Pour in the vegetable stock. Add the cooked nettle tops and stir so they are well mixed in. Roughly chop the watercress and add to the saucepan. Bring to the boil and simmer for 5 minutes. Liquidise the soup, which should be a rich dark green purée. Season with the chilli, salt and pepper and add the milk. Serve with a swirl of cream and a dusting of paprika.

Wear rubber gloves when picking and handling to avoid stings. Once cooked, the sting disappears. Make this soup in spring or early summer for the best flavour.

Salmon Fishcakes

8oz/225g salmon fillet
1lb/450g potatoes cooked, mashed and cooled
2 tablespoons onion or spring onion, finely chopped
2 tablespoons parsley, finely chopped
Grated rind and juice of half a lemon
1 egg, well beaten
2 tablespoons plain flour
Salt and pepper to taste
1oz/25g butter
2 tablespoons olive or sunflower oil

Steam the salmon until cooked (approx. 10 minutes). Put in a mixing bowl and flake, removing any bones. Allow to cool. Then add the mashed potato, onion, parsley and lemon. Use the rest of the lemon for the lemon-wedge garnish. Stir in the beaten egg and season to taste. The mixture is quite soft, but if you wet your hands before forming the cakes it will not stick quite so much. Spread the flour on a plate and as you make each cake (the mixture will provide eight, two per person) roll it in flour mixed with a little extra seasoning. Heat the butter and oil in a large frying pan and fry the cakes on each side until crisp and golden.

Serve immediately with a wedge of lemon and the Spicy Tomato Sauce (overleaf). Alternatively they are delicious with Dill Mayonnaise on p.72.

Richard, the chef at Baddesley Clinton, says that these disappear 'like hot cakes' as fast as he can make them!

Baked Cod on a Spinach Bed with Spicy Tomato Sauce

4 cod steaks or thick pieces of
  fillet of approx. 4oz/125g
  each
12oz/350g frozen leaf spinach,
  defrosted
2 or 3 tablespoons olive oil
Salt, pepper and herbes de
  Provence

SPICY TOMATO SAUCE
1 tablespoon olive oil
1 small onion, finely chopped
1 clove garlic, chopped or
  crushed
Herbes de Provence
1 tablespoon tomato purée
14oz/400g tin chopped
  tomatoes
1 small wineglass of white or
  red wine
1 dessertspoon sugar
Salt and pepper

Preheat oven to 160°C, 325°F, gas mark 3. Brush a table-spoon of olive oil around the inside of a china gratin or quiche dish large enough to take all the ingredients. Squeeze as much of the water out of the spinach as possible and divide it into four round beds the size of the cod portions. Put in the dish and season with salt and pepper. Lay the fish on top, season to taste with salt, pepper and a little of the herbs. Set aside.

To make the spicy tomato sauce, heat the oil in a shallow pan, add the onion and garlic and herbes de Provence to taste (I use a teaspoonful for a good, but not overpowering, flavour) and cook gently until the onion is soft but not coloured, then add the tomato purée, the tinned tomatoes, the wine and the sugar and increase the heat. Bubble the sauce quite fiercely, stirring from time to time until it reduces a little and thickens. Take off the heat, taste and season. Spoon the sauce over the cod steaks, coating them well. Cover the dish with foil and bake approx. 15 minutes.

Serve with plain boiled rice or new potatoes.

Sausage Plait

12oz/350g puff pastry
1 medium onion, peeled and
    finely chopped
1 large leek, chopped
1 eating apple, peeled and
    chopped
1lb/450g pork sausage meat
1 tablespoon tomato purée
1 dessertspoon Worcestershire
    sauce
1 tablespoon mixed chopped
    fresh herbs (a mixture of
    parsley, sage and thyme
    works well)
Salt and pepper
1 egg beaten with some milk to
    glaze

Preheat oven to 200°C, 400°F, gas mark 6. Roll out the pastry to form a large rectangle, approx. 15 in × 10 in/37 cm × 25 cm. Place on a piece of baking paper on a baking sheet (the paper makes it easier to move the plait). Allow to rest while you prepare the filling.

Mix all the other ingredients together. Form into a sausage shape and lay on the pastry sheet, allowing sufficient pastry at the end to seal and sufficient pastry at the side to form the plait. Brush the uncovered pastry with the glaze and cut into strips 1½ in/4 cm wide. Use these strips to form a lattice over the filling. Seal the ends and brush plait with glaze. Bake 30 to 40 minutes, until brown and crisp.

At Baddesley Clinton the plait is served hot, but it makes excellent picnic food eaten cold.

Courgette Roulade

1¼lb/550g courgettes
1 tablespoon sunflower or
    olive oil
1oz/25g plain flour
5 eggs, separated
1 tablespoon Parmesan cheese
Salt and pepper

STUFFING
Use the Spicy Tomato Sauce on
    p.14

Preheat oven to 220°C, 425°F, gas mark 7. Line a Swiss roll tin 8 in × 6 in/20 cm × 15 cm with baking parchment. Grate the courgettes (this is easiest in a food processor). Heat the oil in a pan and gently sauté the courgettes for 5 minutes. Drain them and allow to cool slightly. Stir in the flour and egg yolks. Whip the whites stiffly with a pinch of salt and fold gently into the flour and yolks. Season to taste with salt and pepper. Spread the mixture evenly in the tin and bake for approx. 15 to 20 minutes until golden, risen and firm to the touch. While it is cooking make the tomato sauce.

Cover with a damp cloth as the roulade cools slightly in the tin. This makes it easier to handle. Spread a piece of greaseproof paper with the Parmesan cheese and turn the roulade out of the tin on to the paper. Peel off the baking paper and spread the roulade with two-thirds of the tomato sauce. Then, very gently, using the paper, roll up the roulade and slide it on to a serving dish. Don't worry if it cracks, you can cover it with the remaining sauce if you wish, otherwise use the sauce as a garnish round it.

Mushroom Stroganoff

1 oz/25 g butter
1 tablespoon sunflower oil
1 medium onion, finely chopped
3 sticks celery, finely chopped
Pinch of thyme and one
    crumbled bay leaf
12 oz/350 g button mushrooms
1 tablespoon wholemeal flour
1 teaspoon Marmite
¼ pint/150 ml water or white
    wine
2 tablespoons Greek yoghurt
Salt and pepper to taste
Chopped parsley and paprika to
    garnish

Heat the butter and oil together and sauté the chopped onion and celery with the thyme and bay leaf until soft. Chop the mushrooms into halves or quarters and add to the pan. Add the flour and turn the vegetables so that they are well coated. Cook gently for 5 minutes, then add the Marmite and the wine or water. Cook another 5 minutes, taste to ensure that the flour is cooked and stir in the yoghurt. Reheat gently, stirring all the time so that the sauce does not separate. Serve immediately on a bed of rice garnished with chopped parsley and paprika.

This is a surprisingly rich dish and only needs a green salad as an accompaniment.

Baddesley Apple Cake

CRUMBLE MIXTURE
12 oz/350 g wholemeal flour
12 oz/350 g plain flour
12 oz/350 g butter
4 oz/125 g caster sugar
1 level teaspoon cinnamon

FILLING
1½ lb/675 g cooking apples
2 oz/50 g sultanas
2 oz/50 g brown sugar

Preheat oven to 180°C, 350°F, gas mark 4. Grease a 9 in/ 23 cm springform cake tin. Make the crumble: rub the fat into the two flours sifted together with the cinnamon and stir in the sugar. Alternatively, put all the crumble ingredients into a food processor and process until they resemble coarse breadcrumbs.

Peel and slice the apples. Line the cake tin with two-thirds of the crumble mixture, pressing it down on the base and up round the sides to form a shell. Pack the centre tightly with apple slices, scattering sultanas and brown sugar on them as you go. Top with the rest of the crumble. Bake for approx. 1 hour 20 minutes. Serve warm in slices with ice-cream or pouring cream.

This recipe was found on a card left by the land-girls who worked the farm here during the Second World War. It tastes just as good fifty years on.

BIDDULPH GRANGE GARDEN
STAFFORDSHIRE

Biddulph Grange Garden is a Victorian delight, a treasure house of secret places, beautiful plants, microclimates and surprises. This 'world image' garden was the creation of three passionate gardeners, James and Maria Bateman and their friend, the marine painter Edward Cooke. Between 1849 and 1868 they brought together trees, shrubs and plants from all over the world and re-created their idea of that world within the garden. Besides plants, they used boulders, water, eccentric buildings, topiary and even tree-stumps.

They were all great plantsmen. James fell in love with orchids at an early age, then his attention turned to pines, rhododendrons and azaleas. He became passionately interested in dahlias – the magnificent Dahlia Walk is in the process of restoration. Maria loved lilies, fuchsias and herbaceous plants. Her own sheltered garden near the house has borders planted in her taste. Edward was fascinated by ferns – two of his own houses were called 'The Ferns'. He could not resist designing architectural features. The rock arrangements in the garden, as well as the different buildings, are probably his work.

Nothing is as it seems. The shadows under the great limes of the Lime Avenue are not shadows at all but carefully trained Irish ivy and tree ivy. An imposing topiary entrance leads to the Egyptian temple of the Ape of Thoth, a gloomy, forbidding place containing an alarming statue of the Ape lividly lit from above by ruby glass. The exit is anything but imposing. If you look back when you leave the temple, the façade is of a cosy Cheshire cottage.

Tunnels and hedges screen the next view and, like the Victorian visitors James Bateman encouraged, you have to marvel. The extraordinary stumpery is a path lined with tree roots and stumps planted upside down to display ivies and ferns. Turn a corner from the glen, shady, moist, full of delicate foliage and rocks, and you are in a magical Victorian evocation of China: a landscape of red and green painted, intricately carved temples, a great golden buffalo's statue, a 'willow pattern' bridge across a still pool. The plants here were exciting new discoveries from the Far East when the garden was created. The maples, hostas and tree peonies increase the exotic, secret atmosphere. 'China' is the heart of Biddulph's green world but there is much else, including the Italian Garden, the Pinetum and the Arboretum.

The imposing mansion is not open to visitors, except for the old billiard-room, furnished with Lloyd Loom chairs and small tables where you can refresh yourself with home-made soup and cakes. The specialities of the area, Staffordshire oat-cakes and pikelets, are baked locally in Biddulph.

Cauliflower Cheese Soup

2 oz/50 g butter
1 large onion, finely chopped
12 oz/350 g cauliflower
1 pint/500 ml vegetable stock
1 oz/25 g cornflour
½ pint/250 ml milk
2 oz/50 g grated Cheddar or
    crumbled Stilton cheese
Salt and pepper to taste
1 tablespoon parsley, chopped

Melt the butter in a large saucepan. Add the onion and cook gently until it is soft but not coloured. Add the cauliflower and vegetable stock, bring the mixture to the boil and simmer until the cauliflower breaks into small pieces. Mix the cornflour into a smooth paste with a little of the milk. Add the rest of the milk to the pan. Stir in the cornflour paste and bring to the boil. Reduce the heat immediately and simmer for 5 minutes. Then add the cheese, season to taste with salt and pepper, stir in the parsley and serve immediately.

Staffordshire Oatcakes

8 oz/225 g bread flour
8 oz/225 g fine oatmeal
2 teaspoons salt
½ oz/15 g bakers' yeast
¾ pint/400 ml warm milk
¾ pint/400 ml warm water
Butter for greasing frying pan or
    griddle

To make 16 to 18 × 6–7 in/16–18 cm oatcakes.
Put flour and oatmeal in a bowl with salt. Cream the yeast with a little of the warm milk. Stir into the flour, add the rest of the liquid and beat well with a wooden spoon. If it seems too thick add a little more warm water. Cover the bowl and leave to rise for an hour or so.

Heat a griddle or heavy-based frying pan until very hot. Grease sparingly and make the oatcakes as you would pancakes. Put a ladle of mixture into the pan, cook for a minute or two until bubbles appear in the mixture, then flip over and cook for another minute or two. The oatcakes can be kept warm in a folded damp cloth.

At Biddulph the oatcakes are made by a local baker but the recipe is a secret, so I have adapted this recipe from Elizabeth David's *English Bread and Yeast Cookery*. She describes the oatcakes as 'an intensely local delicacy unheard of north of Leek, unimagined south of Banbury'. The tea-room at Biddulph serves them for lunch with vegetables. They can also be eaten with butter and honey or with bacon and eggs for breakfast.

Malt Loaf

8 oz/225 g self-raising flour
4 oz/125 g sultanas
1 teacup granulated sugar
1 teacup cold milk
2 tablespoons black treacle
1 egg, well beaten

Preheat oven to 150°C, 300°F, gas mark 2. Line a 1 lb/450 g loaf tin with baking parchment. Mix together the flour, sultanas and sugar. Warm the milk and treacle, add to the dry ingredients. Add the egg and beat to a smooth batter. Place in the prepared tin and smooth the top. Bake approx. 1 hour 15 minutes. Remove from the tin and paper and cool on a wire tray.

This loaf is best wrapped in greaseproof paper or foil and kept for two or three days before using. It is moist and fruity and usually served spread with butter.

Nutty Syrup Tart

6 oz/175 g shortcrust pastry
8 oz/225 g golden syrup
5 oz/150 g fresh breadcrumbs
  (approx. 5 slices from a large
  sliced loaf), they can be
  wholemeal or white or a
  mixture of both
1 dessertspoon lemon juice
2 oz/50 g chopped mixed nuts

Preheat oven to 180°C, 350°F, gas mark 4. Line a 10 in/25 cm ovenproof plate with the shortcrust pastry. Place all the ingredients except the nuts into a saucepan and heat *very* gently, stirring all the time. The easiest way to measure golden syrup is to warm it slightly so that it thins and then to pour it into a measuring jug. Do not let it get too hot, because it will catch and burn. Spread on the pastry base. Sprinkle the top with the nuts. Bake for 15 to 20 minutes.

A variation on an old favourite, much requested by visitors to Biddulph.

BUCKLAND ABBEY
DEVON

Buckland Abbey's most famous owner was Sir Francis Drake, the man who defeated the great Spanish Armada – after finishing his game of bowls on Plymouth Hoe. He spent much of his time far from peaceful Buckland Abbey, across the Atlantic exploring, harrying the Spanish fleet and 'privateering' – lying in wait for his prey, capturing the vessel, putting aboard his own crew to sail it home laden with rich cargoes which swelled his own coffers and those of his delighted Queen. Elizabeth I paid off her foreign debts from booty brought home by Drake and some of the balance went to fund the forerunner of the East India Company. Piracy, as the Spanish called it, definitely paid.

At sea, after the fresh provisions had been consumed, Elizabethan sailors lived chiefly on biscuit, salt beef and beer supplemented by rancid cheese and butter. Small wonder that in contemporary accounts of their voyages as much is written about the food they found on board their prizes as the gold and silver. Francis Pretty, sailing in 1596 with Sir Richard Cavendish, comments of a ship taken off

Santiago in Chile that it was 'laden with sugar, molasses, maize, Cordovan skins, montego de porco, many packs of pintados, many Indian coats, some marmalade and one thousand hens'. He adds that this cargo would have been worth £20,000, if only they had captured it 'where they might have sold it'. On this occasion, as much as possible of the cargo was transferred, the rest burnt with the ship and the men and women 'that were not killed' were set ashore.

That was the down side of privateering. Extra mouths to feed were a liability. John Hawkins, Drake's cousin, left half his crew behind to fend for themselves in the West Indies in 1568 with a vague promise to come back and get them in a year or so. He never did.

Hungry men are not faddy. Fresh from the privations of rationed beer and biscuit, these men tried anything. There are accounts of meals of seals, penguins and gulls, mussels, dogfish and limpets, wild hogs, plantains and turtles, cassava roots and all kinds of unknown 'fowls and fruits'. Some new vegetables were accounted delicious: 'these potatoes be the most delicate roots that may be eaten and do far exceed our parsnips or carrots'.

The traditions of Drake's adventurous sailors are being maintained in the restaurant at Buckland. The food is both interesting and innovative. Herbs come from the herb garden, vegetables are local. Recipes have come not just from the excellent cooks, but also from the volunteers, who are producing their own cook book in 1995, Amy at reception and Sally Whitfield, the head gardener.

Carrot and Ginger Soup

1lb/450g carrots
1 medium onion
2oz/50g butter
2½ pints/1.5 litres vegetable stock
½ teaspoon ground ginger
Rind and juice of two oranges
2 tablespoons ground rice
Salt and pepper

Peel carrots and onion and slice thinly. Melt the butter and sauté carrot and onion slices in a large pan for 5 minutes. Add the vegetable stock and ginger. Bring to the boil and simmer for 15 minutes. Add the ground rice, orange juice and rind and simmer for a further 15 minutes. Liquidise, return to the pan, season with salt and pepper to taste and serve piping hot.

Buckland Abbey often serve their soups with Sippets: buttered bread cut into small cubes, placed in a roasting pan, sprinkled with mixed herbs and baked in a low oven until brown and crisp.

Tomato Mousse

6 large tomatoes
1 small onion, peeled and
    chopped fine
1 oz/25 g butter
2 oz/50 g button mushrooms,
    chopped
3-4 basil leaves
1 clove garlic
1 teaspoon sugar
Salt and pepper to taste
1 tablespoon gelatine
¼ pint/150 ml double cream

Plunge tomatoes into boiling water for a minute and skin. Cut in half, de-seed and chop roughly. Melt the butter and sauté the onion for a few minutes until soft. Add the mushrooms, basil leaves, garlic clove, sugar and tomatoes. Stir well and simmer until soft. Remove the garlic clove and purée the mixture. Taste and season accordingly with salt and pepper. Melt the gelatine in a little hot water and stir into the purée. Stir occasionally while it cools. When it is beginning to thicken and set, whip the cream lightly and fold into the mixture, pour into a mould and chill for several hours. Serve with a green salad.

You may need to double the gelatine if the weather is very hot and thundery. South Devon tomatoes have a particularly good flavour. This recipe was given to me by the volunteers at Buckland Abbey. It will be featuring in their own cookery book available from the shop there.

Lentil and Carrot Pâté

5 oz/150 g red lentils
5 oz/150 g carrots, peeled and
    grated
2 oz/50 g onion, peeled and
    finely chopped
2 garlic cloves, peeled and finely
    chopped
2 tablespoons olive oil
1 tablespoon yeast extract
Salt and pepper
Juice of 1 lemon
1 chunk of crystallised ginger
Small pot (approx. 4 oz/100 g)
    Greek yoghurt

Put the lentils and carrots in a saucepan and just cover with water. Bring to the boil, reduce heat and simmer until soft, approx. 20 minutes. Heat the oil and sauté the onion and garlic for 5 minutes. Take off the heat. Drain the lentils and carrots and add to the onion and garlic. Mash well and season with yeast extract, pepper and lemon juice. Cool and then chill. When the lentil mixture is completely cold, liquidise the ginger with the yoghurt and blend in. Pack the mixture into ramekins and serve with melba toast or crudités.

Lentils are rich in protein, carrots in vitamins A and C. Not only tasty and a beautiful colour, but healthy as well.

Braised Rabbit with Prunes

1 dessertspoon sunflower oil
1 oz/25 g butter
8 rabbit pieces
Dijon mustard
20 pickling onions, peeled
4 oz/125 g smoked bacon, diced
1 teaspoon dried thyme
Approx. ½ pint/250 ml dry
   white wine
8 pitted prunes
2 tablespoons brandy
Salt and pepper

Preheat oven to 180°C, 350°F, gas mark 4. Melt the oil and butter in a frying pan and brown the rabbit pieces on all sides. Remove with a slotted spoon, spread all over with Dijon mustard and put in a casserole. Brown the onions and bacon and add to the casserole with the thyme. Cover with wine, season with salt and freshly ground pepper. Cook for about an hour, then add the brandy and the prunes. Cook for a further 30 minutes. By this time the rabbit should be really tender.

Keith Floyd is the cook who originated this recipe which is served at Christmas feasts at Buckland. In the Middle Ages rabbits were the exclusive preserve of the nobility and cost the equivalent of £20 each.

Chicken in Hocchee

4 chicken breasts
4 oz/125 g green grapes
2 tablespoons mixed chopped
   fresh parsley and sage (if you
   have to use dried sage, use
   only about a quarter sage to
   parsley)
1 clove garlic
½ pint/250 ml chicken stock
1 small glass white wine
½ teaspoon caster sugar
½ teaspoon ground cinnamon
Garnish of chopped parsley and
   a few grapes

Pip the grapes if necessary, reserving a few for garnishing. Mix the rest with the garlic and the herbs and stuff the chicken breasts with the mixture. Pin each breast into a neat parcel with a cocktail stick and place in a dish which just holds them. Add the stock and wine and cover the dish with foil. Simmer until tender (about 45 minutes). Remove the breasts and place on a warm serving dish. Sprinkle with the sugar and cinnamon mixed together, the chopped parsley and grapes. Serve with the cooking juices as a gravy.

This is a modern adaptation of a medieval or Tudor recipe: 'Take chykens and scald them, take parsel and sawge, without any other erbes, take garlec and grapes, and stoppe the chikens ful, and seeth them in good broth, so that they may esly be boyled thereinne. Messe them and cast thereto powdor-douce [a mixture of mild spices].'

Mixed Vegetable Burgundy Casserole

MARINADE
¾ pint/400 ml red wine
4 tablespoons brandy
Sprig of fresh rosemary
12 whole peppercorns, crushed
12 juniper berries, crushed
1 teaspoon sea salt
1 teaspoon mustard powder

CASSEROLE
4 oz/125 g dried apricots
4 oz/125 g dried chick-peas
4 oz/125 g dried chestnuts
1 large aubergine
2 large onions, peeled and sliced
2 large carrots, peeled and sliced
10 cloves garlic, peeled and
  sliced
2 tablespoons olive oil
1 pint/500 ml vegetable stock
1 tablespoon paprika
Zest and juice 1 lemon
1 tablespoon brown sugar
Salt and pepper to taste

This recipe must be started three days in advance.

DAY ONE Mix all the ingredients of the marinade together and add the apricots. Put chick-peas and chestnuts into water to soak separately.

DAY TWO Boil chick-peas and chestnuts in plenty of water until tender. Drain and add to marinade.

DAY THREE Chop aubergine into cubes. Sprinkle with salt and leave for 2 hours, turning occasionally. Rinse, drain, pat dry and add to the marinade. Heat the oil in a heavy saucepan or casserole and cook the sliced vegetables for a minute or two, then add the marinade, its contents and the vegetable stock. Bring to the boil and simmer for 1½ hours. Remove from heat.* Remove vegetables with a slotted spoon. Set aside and keep warm while you finish the sauce. Return the pan to the heat. Add the paprika, lemon zest and sugar. Boil the mixture rapidly to reduce it to approx. ½ pint/300 ml of liquid. It will now be thick and sticky. Return the vegetables to the pan, coat with the sauce and serve.

Everything can be done in advance up to this stage*. So, although it is a recipe that involves considerable preparation, it is really quite practical. At Buckland, this recipe is served as a vegetarian alternative to turkey on Christmas menus. It would also be a wonderful accompaniment to roast turkey.

Bulgur Shepherd's Pie

2oz/50g bulgur wheat
2 tablespoons olive oil
4oz/100g onion, chopped
1 clove garlic
2oz/50g carrots, peeled and
    sliced
4oz/125g courgettes, chopped
6oz/175g button mushrooms
6fl oz/175ml vegetable stock
8oz/225g tin chopped tomatoes
2 tablespoons vegetable purée
    (use passata purée if not
    available)
2 tablespoons chopped parsley
Salt and pepper to taste

TOPPING
1lb/450g potatoes
2oz/50g butter, melted
2 tablespoons warm milk
4oz/125g grated Cheddar cheese

A pie for vegetarian shepherds! Preheat oven to 200°C, 400°F, gas mark 6. Cover bulgur wheat with water, bring to the boil and cook for 10 minutes until all the water is absorbed. Heat oil in a saucepan and sauté onion, garlic and carrots for 5 minutes, add courgettes and mushrooms and cook for a further 5 minutes. Add the vegetable stock, chopped tomatoes, vegetable purée and parsley to the sautéed vegetables and season to taste. Add the bulgur wheat and mix well in the saucepan. It should be liquid but thick. Pour into a gratin dish.

Peel and dice the potatoes, boil until tender, drain and mash until smooth with warm milk and melted butter. Top the vegetable mixture with the mash, fluff up with a fork and cover with grated cheese. Bake until the top is golden brown, approx. 15 to 20 minutes.

Abbot's Fruit Pudding

1oz/25g sago
½ pint/250ml milk
8oz/225g breadcrumbs
8oz/225g mixed fruit
6oz/175g dark brown sugar
1 teaspoon bicarbonate of soda
1 teaspoon mixed spice

Soak the sago overnight in the milk. Butter a 2pint/1250ml pudding basin. In a bowl large enough to take all the ingredients, dissolve the bicarbonate of soda in a little extra milk, add all the rest of the ingredients, mix well and put in the pudding basin. Cover with a layer of greaseproof paper and foil and steam for 2 hours. Serve with an Egg Custard Sauce (opposite).

Sally Whitfield, head gardener at Buckland Abbey, was given this recipe by Annie, a local lady, who is now over 90.

Egg Custard Sauce

½ pint/250 ml full cream milk or
    single cream
3 egg yolks
1 level tablespoon sugar
1 level teaspoon cornflour
2 drops vanilla essence

Heat the milk or cream in a saucepan to almost boiling. Blend the egg yolks, cornflour, sugar and vanilla essence together in a small bowl. Then pour on the hot milk or cream, stirring all the time, and return to the saucepan. Heat very gently, still stirring, until the sauce has thickened.

This sauce recipe comes from Anglesey Abbey near Cambridge and appeared in the first *Book of National Trust Recipes*. It is so popular, wherever it is served, that I have included it again, the only recipe to have that distinction.

Walnut Cheesecake

3 oz/75 g butter
2 oz/50 g sugar
6 oz/175 g digestive biscuits,
    finely crushed
8 oz/225 g curd cheese
3 eggs, separated
4 tablespoons golden syrup
1 heaped tablespoon plain flour
6 tablespoons whipping cream
2 oz/50 g caster sugar
3 oz/75 g chopped walnuts
Walnut halves and icing sugar

Preheat oven to 160°C, 325°C, gas mark 3. Brush an 8 in/20 cm springform tin with vegetable oil. Melt the butter and sugar in a saucepan and stir in the biscuit crumbs. Press evenly over the bottom of the tin. Chill while you make the topping.

Soften the cheese in a large mixing bowl. Beat in the egg yolks, golden syrup, flour and cream. Whisk the egg whites until stiff, then whisk the sugar into the whites. Fold this mixture into the cheese mixture, together with the walnut pieces. Spread over the biscuit-crumb base. Arrange walnut halves on the top and place in the oven. Bake approx. 1½ hours, until firm but still spongy to the touch. Turn off the oven, open the door and leave the cheesecake to cool in the oven for an hour. Then chill, still in the tin, for 2 to 3 hours. Run a knife around the inside of the tin before carefully removing the sides. Dust the cake with icing sugar and serve with either a fruit sauce or more cream.

Buckland Abbey Restaurant cheesecakes are famous. A different version is on the menu every day. This was the first time I had come across one using walnuts – it is delicious.

Carrot and Nut Cake

9 oz/250 g carrots, peeled and
    coarsely grated
4 eggs, separated
7 oz/200 g soft light brown sugar
4 oz/125 g 'ready to eat' dried
    apricots
4 oz/125 g brazil nuts, roughly
    chopped
4 oz/125 g hazelnuts
1½ oz/40 g sunflower seeds
Grated rind of 1 orange plus
    1 tablespoon orange juice
4 oz/125 g wholemeal flour
1 level teaspoon baking powder
1 level teaspoon ground
    cinnamon

Preheat oven to 180°C, 350°F, gas mark 4. Grease and line, or line with baking paper, a 9 in/23 cm loose-bottomed cake tin. Dry the grated carrots with kitchen paper or drain in a sieve for 15 minutes. Whisk the egg yolks with sugar until thick and creamy. Stir in carrots, apricots, 3 oz/75 g of brazil nuts, the hazelnuts, 1 oz/25 g of sunflower seeds, orange rind and juice. Sift together the flour, baking powder and cinnamon and stir into the carrot mixture. Beat the egg whites until stiff and fold into the mixture. Pour the mixture into the tin and bake for approx. 40 minutes. Sprinkle on remaining nuts and seeds and bake for a further 30 minutes. Leave cake to cool in the tin for 10 minutes, then remove and cool on a wire tray. Wrap the cake in greaseproof paper or foil and store for two days to allow it to mature.

Amy's Mincemeat

3 lb/1350 g cooking apples,
    peeled, cored and finely
    chopped
Juice and finely grated rind
    1 orange
Juice and finely grated rind
    1 lemon
1 pint/500 ml medium sweet
    cider
1 lb/450 g brown sugar
1 teaspoon ground cinnamon
1 teaspoon grated nutmeg
1 teaspoon ground cloves
1 lb/450 g raisins
1 lb/450 g currants
8 oz/225 g glacé cherries, halved
4 fl oz/100 ml rum

Makes about 6 lb/3 kg

Put the apples, juices and cider in a large saucepan or pre-serving pan. Bring to the boil, reduce the heat and simmer for 10 minutes. Stir in the sugar, cinnamon, nutmeg, cloves, raisins and currants. When the sugar has dissolved, simmer the mixture for a further 15 minutes. Remove the pan from the heat and stir in the glacé cherries. Allow the mixture to cool completely and stir in the rum. Pack into glass jam jars and cover.

Since this contains no suet, it is suitable for vegetarians. Home-made mincemeat rewards the effort of making it; both the texture and the taste are quite different from the commercial product.

This recipe was provided by Amy, who works on the reception at Buckland.

Locket's Savoury

6–8 slices wholemeal bread
Butter
1 large bunch of watercress
3–4 large ripe pears
6–8 slices Devon Blue cheese
(Stilton or Blue Cheshire
make good substitutes)

Preheat oven to 190°C, 375°F, gas mark 5. Remove the crusts from the bread, toast lightly, butter and lay out on a baking tray. Destalk and chop the watercress and sprinkle thickly on the slices. Peel the pears, cut in half and de-core. Lay one pear half on each slice of toast. Cover the pear halves with cheese slices. Bake for approx. 10 minutes. Serve immediately.

Pears and blue cheese are an unbeatable combination, particularly in Devon where they are both produced locally.

Home-made Orange Cordial

1 lemon
3 oranges
1½ lb/675 g granulated or caster
sugar
1 oz/25 g citric acid
2 pints/1250 ml boiling water

Rub the zest from the lemon and oranges, cut the fruit in half and squeeze out the juice. Chop the shells into chunks. Put sugar, citric acid, lemon and orange zest, juice and chunks of shell in a large bowl. Add the boiling water, stir to help the sugar dissolve and leave to cool and stand, preferably overnight. Strain to remove lemon and orange pieces. Pour cordial into a jug or clean bottles and store in a refrigerator. Use diluted as required. The cordial can be kept for two or three weeks.

Mulled Wine

1 orange
12/14 whole cloves
1¾ pints/1 litre red wine
1¾ pints/1 litre lemonade
⅔ teacup brown sugar
⅔ teacup orange juice
1 × 6 in/1 × 15 cm cinnamon stick

Stud the orange with cloves and cut in half. Place all the ingredients in a large saucepan and bring *very slowly* almost to a simmer. Serve hot but do not allow to boil.

This mull is rather like a hot sangria – the Spanish element seems particularly appropriate, given Francis Drake's connections with Buckland Abbey.

CALKE ABBEY
DERBYSHIRE

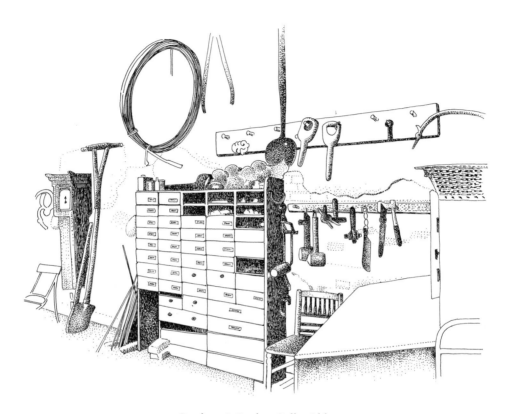

Gardener's Bothy, Calke Abbey

To conserve or to restore – which is the correct role for the National Trust? At Calke Abbey the Trust has come down resoundingly on the side of conservation. This is particularly appropriate since the Harpur Crewe family were themselves conservators long before conservation was valued. In the eighteenth century contemporary commentators noted with amazement the fondness of Sir Henry Harpur, the 'Isolated [7th] Baronet', for watching wild animals. Eccentricity, isolation and a deep identification with the natural world were to be a continuing characteristic of the family. They were also renowned as collectors and for never throwing anything away.

Calke Abbey is the house 'where time has stood still'. Apart from the wear and tear of time, little has changed since 1886 when Sir Vauncey Harpur Crewe, the last

Baronet and the last great collector, inherited the house. It is his world that Calke today reflects. His predecessors had already filled the house with natural history collections, he added yet more. The Saloon, a huge room in the centre of the house, is full of display cases of 'curiosities' still labelled in Sir Vauncey's spidery writing.

Besides 1,500 birds' eggs, 10,000 butterflies, moths, beetles, bees, flies and wasps, shells, fossils, stuffed birds and animals, polished stones and minerals, the buildings, cupboards and drawers of Calke yielded a treasure trove reflecting the eclectic interests of the family. Sir Harry, the 6th Baronet, started the collection of animal portraits in the eighteenth century. The fine collection of carriages is the result of Sir Vauncey's dislike of the motor car. He refused to allow cars in the park. Guests had to leave their cars at the Lodge and wait for a carriage to collect them. Drawers revealed dolls carefully wrapped, sets of lead soldiers in mint condition. Wooden trunks contained complete wardrobes of nineteenth-century children's clothes. In Sir Vauncey's bedroom collections of walking sticks and purses and hundreds of trinkets and souvenirs jostled more birds' eggs and butterflies.

Perhaps the most spectacular survival of all is the 1715 State Bed hung with brilliantly coloured Chinese silks. The colours are as vivid as the day they were embroidered because the bed was never put up. No room was large enough to take it, so it stayed in its box, a well-kept secret like Calke itself, until the Trust took over.

The Harpur Crewe family fought change by withdrawing from the world beyond Calke. Now the world comes to Calke to marvel at a bygone age, miraculously preserved. Move into the modern age when you need refreshment. The restaurant is a handsome room created from the byre and cattle sheds. The furniture and lighting is modern, underfloor heating cossets twentieth-century visitors. Local ingredients are important, recipes are imaginative. Puddings are famous, the Calke Abbey Desserters' Club meets regularly to sample a selection.

Spicy Lentil Soup

1 oz/25 g butter
*1 medium onion, peeled and
    chopped*
1 clove garlic, finely chopped
1 teaspoon cumin
½ teaspoon ginger
*1 green pepper, de-seeded and
    diced*
*1 red pepper, de-seeded and
    diced*
1 bay leaf
1 pint/500 ml vegetable stock
8 oz/225 g red lentils
½ pint/250 ml milk

Melt the butter and sauté the chopped onion until soft. Add the garlic, cumin and ginger, cook for a few minutes more. Stir in the diced peppers, bay leaf, vegetable stock and lentils. Bring to the boil and simmer until cooked. Remove the bay leaf, add the milk and reheat to just below boiling.

Served with crusty French or naan bread, this soup is a meal in itself.

Courgette and Tomato Soup

1 tablespoon olive oil
1 onion, peeled and chopped
*2 cloves garlic, peeled and
    chopped*
*14 oz/400 g tin chopped
    tomatoes*
1 lb/450 g courgettes, chopped
1 dessertspoon tomato purée
*1 dessertspoon chopped fresh
    basil (use 1 teaspoon dried
    basil if fresh is not available)*
1 tablespoon wine vinegar
1 teaspoon sugar
1½ pints/750 ml vegetable stock
Salt and pepper to taste
Extra basil to garnish

Heat the oil in a large saucepan and sauté the onion and garlic until soft. Add tomatoes, courgettes, tomato purée, basil, vinegar, sugar and stock. Simmer until courgettes are tender (approx. 10 minutes). Purée and season to taste. Serve garnished with a little extra chopped basil.

Chicken with Garlic Sauce

4 chicken joints
12 cloves garlic
1 tablespoon sunflower oil
2oz/50g sultanas
1 glass white wine
1 tablespoon red wine vinegar
1 dessertspoon Dijon mustard
1 tablespoon tomato purée
¼ pint/150ml single cream
Salt and pepper

GARNISH
2oz/50g sunflower seeds
Handful of chopped parsley

Brush the chicken joints and the garlic cloves, still in their skin, with sunflower oil and roast until completely cooked. Put the cooked joints on a serving plate and keep warm in the oven while making the sauce.

Retrieve the garlic cloves. Pop the cooked garlic out of its skins and mash or purée. In a small saucepan simmer together the sultanas, white wine, vinegar, mustard and tomato purée until quite thick. Blend in the puréed garlic and cream and reheat gently, stirring so the mixture does not separate. Season with salt and pepper to taste and pour over the cooked chicken. Garnish with the sunflower seeds and parsley.

This may seem a lot of garlic, but cooked in this way the flavour is quite delicious, not overwhelming at all. As well as reputedly protecting you from the evil eye, garlic is very good for health!

Venison Casseroled with Apricots

2oz/50g dried apricots
3oz/75g butter
2 medium onions, peeled and
    sliced
1¼lb/550g venison cut into
    large cubes
2 tablespoons flour
1 dessertspoon crushed juniper
    berries
Pepper and salt to taste
½ pint/250ml apple or apricot
    juice
½ pint/250ml red wine

GARNISH
Chopped parsley
Greek yoghurt

Soak the apricots in cold water overnight.

Preheat oven to 160°C, 325°F, gas mark 3. In a sauté pan, melt the butter and sauté the sliced onions until soft and golden. Take out with a slotted spoon and place in a casserole. Now sauté the venison until brown and add to the onions with any cooking juices from the sauté pan. Mix the flour with the crushed juniper berries and salt and pepper to taste. Sprinkle over the meat and onions and turn them well in the flour mixture. Place the casserole in the oven for 10 minutes. Meanwhile heat the juice and wine gently. Remove casserole from oven, add juice, wine and drained apricots. Stir and return to oven. Cook gently for at least 2 hours, or until meat is tender. This may take longer if the venison was wild rather than farmed.

To serve, sprinkle with parsley and hand round a bowl of yoghurt separately for guests to add if they wish.

Haslet

1lb/450g minced shoulder of
　pork – not sausage meat
5oz/150g brown or white
　breadcrumbs
1 dessertspoon finely chopped
　fresh sage (use 1 teaspoon
　dried sage if fresh is not
　available)
½ teaspoon mace
4oz/125g onion, finely chopped
Salt and pepper to taste

Preheat oven to 180°C, 350°F, gas mark 4. Either line a 1lb/450g loaf tin with baking paper or grease it well. Soak breadcrumbs in a little water, then add to the rest of the ingredients in a mixing bowl and mix well together. Season to taste and pack into the tin. Bake uncovered for 1 hour. Serve hot accompanied by Spicy Tomato Sauce (p.14).

Local bakers in Derbyshire serve Haslet cold as a sandwich filling. Recipes for Haslet can be found in several English counties; I have come across a similar recipe from Hampshire. The name comes from the Old French 'Hastelet' which means entrails or innards, but here it seems to refer to the finely chopped mixture.

Fruit Crumble Sponge

1½lb/675g prepared fruit
4oz/125g butter
4oz/125g caster sugar
2 eggs
Few drops vanilla essence
6oz/175g plain flour
1 teaspoon baking powder
2oz/50g cornflour
2oz/50g ground almonds

TOPPING
4oz/125g butter
2oz/50g caster sugar
2oz/50g ground almonds
2oz/50g cornflour

Choose your fruit according to season: apples or pears, peeled and sliced, or plums stoned and cut into halves in the autumn; soft fruits such as gooseberries, blackcurrants or raspberries, in the summer.

Preheat oven to 180°C, 350°F, gas mark 4. Butter a deep ovenproof dish. Cream the butter and sugar together until pale and fluffy. Beat in the eggs and vanilla essence. Fold in the flour, baking powder, cornflour and almonds sifted together. Spread the mixture on the bottom of the dish. Cover with the prepared fruit. In a large bowl rub together all the topping ingredients and sprinkle over the fruit. Bake for approx. 1 to 1½ hours. Serve warm with cream.

Apple and Cinnamon Cake

8oz/225g margarine
8oz/225g dark soft brown sugar
3 eggs
4 tablespoons apple juice
1lb/450g self-raising flour
3oz/75g sultanas
1 large Bramley cooking apple

TOPPING
4oz/125g butter
6oz/150g plain flour
1 teaspoon cinnamon
6oz/175g demerara sugar

Preheat oven to 160°C, 325°F, gas mark 3. If you are going to make this to serve warm as a pudding, butter a 2 pint/1150ml ovenproof dish. If you are going to serve it cold as a cake, line an 8in/20cm springform tin with baking paper.

Cream the margarine with the sugar until light and fluffy. Beat the eggs well and add to the mixture alternating with sifted flour, apple juice and sultanas. Put two-thirds of the mixture into the dish or tin. Peel and slice the apple and lay on the mixture. Spread the remaining mixture over the apple slices.

For the topping: sift the flour with the cinnamon and rub in the butter until the mixture resembles fine breadcrumbs. Stir in the sugar and scatter over the top of the cake. Bake for approx. an hour, or until a skewer plunged into the middle of the cake comes out clean.

This is a favourite of the 'Calke Abbey Desserters'.

Ashby Statutes

4oz/125g butter
3oz/75g caster sugar
8oz/225g plain flour
½ teaspoon baking powder
1 egg, well beaten
4oz/125g mixed dried fruit and/
   or nuts

Either use mixed dried fruit or make your own mixture – I find finely chopped cherries, crystallised ginger and walnut pieces are a good combination.

Preheat oven to 180°C, 350°F, gas mark 4. Either grease a baking sheet well or line it with baking paper. Cream the butter or margarine with the sugar until pale and fluffy. Sift flour and baking powder, mix with the fruit and nuts and add to the mixture alternately with the egg to form a stiff dough. Roll out on a floured surface approx. ⅓in/1cm thick and cut into 3in/7cm rounds. Bake for about 15 to 20 minutes, until nicely brown. Leave to cool on the baking sheet for a few minutes and sprinkle with caster sugar.

Ashby Statutes are also called Langley Wakes Cakes. Derbyshire villages marked their annual Wakes or Fairs Week in July and August by baking their own versions.

CLIVEDEN
BUCKINGHAMSHIRE

High above the Thames stands Cliveden, home for centuries of the rich, powerful and famous. The mansion is set in acres of elegant formal gardens and parkland, its magnificent vistas and green lawns bounded by steep slopes of hanging woods which drop to the Thames far below.

There have been three houses on the site since George Villiers, 2nd Duke of Buckingham, built the first house just after the restoration of King Charles II in 1660. Villiers was a hugely wealthy courtier and an influential politician, who wrote poetry, plays and satires. He was also a notorious lover who eloped with Anna Maria, Countess of Shrewsbury. Her husband pursued them and Villiers killed him in the subsequent duel, while Anna Maria, dressed as a page boy, held his horse.

This tangle of love and politics is echoed in Cliveden's last scandal. In 1961 while sunbathing by the swimming pool, John Profumo, then Secretary of State for War, first glimpsed the beautiful Christine Keeler. Unfortunately it was the height of the Cold War, she was already sharing her favours with a Russian diplomat and Profumo's infatuation with her almost brought down the Conservative government of the time.

Cliveden's most famous chatelaine, Nancy Astor, was both a beautiful woman and, as the first woman to take her seat in Parliament, a formidable politician. She fought a fierce by-election to become the Member for Plymouth in her husband's place when he inherited his father's title and seat in the House of Lords. Between the two world wars, politicians of all parties, diplomats, writers and entertainers, as well as family and friends flocked to Nancy's house parties and dinners. The comedienne, Joyce Grenfell was Nancy's niece. She spent Christmas at Cliveden as a child and described with affection the rituals of present-giving, carol singers and tea with her formidable aunt 'presiding over the tea table'.

The mansion is now a luxurious hotel, so the parties continue. You can visit some of the rooms and see Nancy still presiding in John Singer Sargent's magnificent portrait of her which hangs above the fireplace in the hall.

The National Trust restaurant at Cliveden is in a white-painted conservatory to the east of the house. Lunches and teas are served among huge pots of geraniums and hanging-baskets of flowers. Vegetarian dishes have long been a speciality and there are several tasty recipes here. I am sure Nancy Astor would have loved the fish terrine which tastes delicious and looks wonderful, a perfect dish for even the grandest party.

Smoked Salmon, Prawn and Chive Terrine

8 oz/225 g smoked salmon, cut
  into long strips
8 oz/225 g cooked and peeled
  prawns
Rind and juice of a lemon
Freshly ground pepper
8 fl oz/225 ml mayonnaise
8 fl oz/225 ml double cream
1 tablespoon gelatine
2 tablespoons freshly chopped
  chives

GARNISH
Sliced cucumber
Fresh dill

Line an oiled terrine or loaf tin, approx. 9 in × 5 in/23 cm × 13 cm with the strips of salmon. In a food processor, combine the rest of the salmon (you should still have about half the original quantity left), 6 oz/175 g of prawns, the lemon rind and juice, pepper, mayonnaise and cream. Process just sufficiently for the mixture to be evenly chopped. Test for seasoning, it may need a little salt. Pour 2 fl oz/60 ml of cold water into a mug or small bowl and set it in a pan of water. Sprinkle the gelatine into the mug and heat until the gelatine is dissolved. Add the melted gelatine to the mixture in the processor and process just long enough to mix thoroughly. Turn the mixture into a bowl and stir in the remaining prawns and chopped chives. Pour into the loaf tin. Smooth the top, cover with cling film, weight slightly and refrigerate overnight.

To unmould, stand the terrine in hot water for a few seconds, then invert on to a serving dish. Garnish with sliced cucumber and fresh dill.

Nutty Scotch Eggs

6 eggs, hardboiled
12 oz/350 g chopped, toasted
  nuts
6 oz/175 g fresh breadcrumbs,
  white or brown
1 teaspoon mixed herbs
6 fl oz/175 ml Marmite stock
Egg and milk wash
More breadcumbs (final
  coating)
Oil for deep frying

Mix the nuts, breadcrumbs and herbs together. Stir in Marmite stock and mix well to give a sticky paste. Use this to make a thick layer around each egg. Allow to rest a few minutes. Then dip each coated egg in egg wash and roll in more breadcrumbs. Heat oil in a deep fryer or wok and fry the eggs until golden. Drain on paper towels.

Vegetable Filo Layer Pie

8 oz/225 g broccoli, divided into florets
8 oz/225 g carrots, peeled and chopped
8 oz/225 g cauliflower, divided into florets
8 oz/225 g butter
2 oz/50 g flour
1 pint/500 ml milk
7½ oz/215 g approx. tin of sweetcorn
Salt and pepper to taste
1 packet filo pastry

Preheat oven to 180°C, 350°F, gas mark 4. Blanch the broccoli, carrots and cauliflower. Make a white sauce with 2 oz/50 g of the butter and all the flour and milk. Stir in sweetcorn and season to taste with pepper and salt.

Melt the remainder of the butter and use to brush the sheets of filo on one side as you make up the pie. Line an oblong gratin dish, approx. 10 in × 8 in/254 cm × 203 cm, with four layers of buttered filo, hanging the ends over the top of the dish. Layer up the pie as follows: first broccoli florets; cover these with chopped carrots (seasoning as you go); spread with the sweetcorn sauce; and finish with cauliflower. Fold the overhanging pieces over the pie and put more buttered filo on top of this to hold it in place. Brush with any remaining butter. If you wish, score the top with a knife to make it easier to divide into portions when cooked. Bake 45 minutes, until puffy and golden.

Cheesy Spinach, Tomato and Onion Pie

1 lb/450 g spinach, blanched and chopped
2 oz/50 g butter
2 oz/50 g plain flour
½ pint/250 ml creamy milk
½ pint/250 ml vegetable stock
6 oz/175 g mature Cheddar, grated
8 oz/225 g tomatoes, roughly chopped
1 medium onion, roughly chopped
1 dessertspoon fresh herbs, chopped
8 oz/225 g shortcrust pastry
Egg and milk to glaze the top

Preheat oven to 180°C, 350°F, gas mark 4. Butter a pie dish large enough to take all the ingredients. Spread the spinach in the bottom. Make a béchamel sauce with the butter, flour, milk and stock and use this to cover the spinach. Sprinkle on the grated cheese. Top with the tomatoes, onion and herbs mixed together. Roll out the pastry and cover the pie. Use any offcuts for decoration, glaze and bake for 30 to 40 minutes, or until the top is crisp and golden.

Garlic Mushroom Nests

4 large wholemeal rolls
2 oz/50 g butter
½ small onion
2 rashers streaky bacon, diced
1 lb/450 g button mushrooms
¼ pint/150 ml single cream
1 tablespoon chopped parsley

This recipe is based on an idea provided by Nigel Slater. Preheat oven to 180°C, 350°F, gas mark 4. Cut the top off each roll and scoop out the crumb to leave a shell. Melt the butter in a frying-pan and use some to paint the inside and outside of the roll shells. Put them on a baking sheet and place in the hot oven to crisp while you prepare the mushroom filling.

Finely chop the onion and fry until soft in the remaining butter. Add the bacon, sauté for a couple of minutes and add the button mushrooms halved or quartered according to size. Cook gently for 5 minutes, then add the cream, stir well and fill the roll shells. Garnish with chopped parsley and serve immediately.

A good light lunch with a green side salad.

Basil, Garlic and Cream Sauce for Pasta

1 dessertspoon olive oil
1 oz/25 g butter
1 small onion, finely chopped
3 cloves garlic, finely chopped
1 × 14 oz/400 g tin chopped
   tomatoes
2 dessertspoons tomato purée
1 teaspoon sugar
Pinch of oregano
Salt and pepper
1 packet fresh basil
¼ pint/150 ml single cream

GARNISH
Parmesan cheese

Melt the oil and butter together and sauté the onion and garlic gently until soft but not brown. Add the tomatoes, tomato purée, sugar and oregano. Bring to boil, then simmer until reduced by about a quarter. Season to taste with salt and pepper. Chop the basil finely and add three-quarters to the mixture with the cream. Reheat the sauce very gently until it is just boiling and serve immediately with tagliatelle. Scatter the remaining basil over the top. Freshly grated Parmesan is a perfect finishing touch.

Icky Sticky Pudding

½ pint/250ml water
6oz/175g chopped dates
1 teaspoon bicarbonate of soda
2oz/50g butter
6oz/175g caster sugar
2 eggs
6oz/175g self-raising flour
½ teaspoon vanilla essence

Preheat oven to 180°C, 350°F, gas mark 4. Either grease well or line with baking paper a deep 8in/20cm dish or tin.

Boil the chopped dates in the water. Remove from heat, add bicarbonate of soda and allow to cool. Cream butter and sugar together until light and fluffy, add the eggs, beating well on each addition. Stir in the cooled date mixture and finally fold in the flour and vanilla essence. Pour into the prepared tin and bake for 35 to 40 minutes. Serve hot with single cream or Caramel Sauce (below).

Caramel Sauce

7oz/200g soft brown sugar
6 tablespoons double cream
4oz/125g butter
½ teaspoon vanilla essence

Mix all the ingredients together and heat gently until the sugar is dissolved and the butter melted. Then boil for 5 minutes and the sauce is ready to serve. (Using a non-stick pan will help to stop the sauce burning.)

A calorific treat – very popular with Cliveden visitors.

ERDDIG
CLWYD

It is entirely appropriate that visitors to Erddig begin their tour in the estate yard, almost as if they, too, are a part of the Yorkes' extended family of devoted, long-serving staff. Erddig is a house where an exploration of the family's relationship with the servants can be as fascinating as the treasures that the house contains. Philip Yorke III, the endearingly eccentric last owner who gave the house to the National Trust in 1973, always insisted that Erddig was their home just as much as it was the home of the generations of Yorkes whom they served. He would probably even have included his 'gardeners', the pet sheep and goats who ate their way through the overgrown garden.

Over the years the Yorkes immortalised this community in paintings, photographs and verse. The eighteenth- and nineteenth-century oil paintings are all but one of men: carpenters, a woodman, gamekeeper, blacksmith, butcher, even a handsome negro coachboy. Jane Ebrell, housemaid, described by Philip Yorke I as 'spider brusher to the master', is the sole female servant depicted. However, above stairs, in the Long Gallery, a much-beloved lady's maid, Betty Ratcliffe, has made her own memorials in exquisite mother-of-pearl models. Housekeepers, nannies and cooks feature in the many photographs which line the basement corridor.

The servants' quarters we see today are mostly unaltered from the 1770s and reflect the unusually informal relationship between 'upstairs' and 'below stairs'. It never bothered the Yorkes that the Servants' Hall looked out over the entrance courtyard. The New Kitchen, built by Philip I in 1774, is the heart of their busy world. It is a wonderful room, architecturally as grand as any at Erddig.

In contrast to this light, spacious workplace are the cramped attic bedrooms. The Yorkes' relationship with their staff was not perfect. They never paid the highest wages, there were failures. In 1787 Philip Yorke I wrote more in sorrow than in anger to John Caesar, his steward, with evidence of fraud. In 1908 Mrs Penketh, a pretty but unreliable housekeeper with a weakness for tippling sherry and whisky, was up before the local magistrates also charged with embezzlement.

There is, however, no question that all the Yorkes preserved a tradition of interest in and concern for their extended family which is still reflected in the attitude of those who work at Erddig. Everybody has their role. Of course part of that role is the preservation of the past, but the estate is still a working estate. The day I was there, the joiners' lathes were turning, the blacksmith's forge was active. In the garden a motor mower has replaced Philip III's pets, but it is still possible for visitors to Erddig to experience this sense of community.

Enthusiasm and a respect for tradition are the hallmarks of the cooking in the Hay Loft Restaurant. Leeks, national vegetable of Wales, feature, as does Bara Brith, Wales's own teabread.

Cream of Leek and Parsley Soup

1 oz/25 g butter
1 medium onion, finely chopped
1 medium potato, peeled and
    diced
1 lb/450 g leeks, chopped
1¾ pints/1 litre vegetable stock
¼ pint/150 ml single cream
1 tablespoon fresh parsley,
    finely chopped

Melt the butter in a large saucepan, add the vegetables and sauté for a few minutes. Add the stock, bring to the boil, reduce the heat and simmer until cooked. Cool slightly, then blend to a smooth consistency. Reheat to just below boiling, add the cream and parsley and serve immediately.

Leeks, the national vegetable of Wales, are worn as an alternative to a daffodil in buttonholes on 1 March, St David's Day.

Lentil Croquettes

8 oz/225 g red lentils
1 teaspoon vegetable oil
4 oz/125 g Cheddar cheese,
    grated
2 tablespoons crunchy peanut
    butter
2 oz/50 g fresh brown
    breadcrumbs
1 tablespoon parsley, chopped
    fine
Squeeze of lemon juice
1 teaspoon Marmite
Salt and pepper to taste
Beaten egg and extra fresh
    breadcrumbs
Vegetable oil

Rinse the lentils, then cook in a large pan with plenty of water. Skim off any scum as they come to the boil. Add the oil and simmer until soft. Drain and cool. As they cool, the lentils will thicken. Add the cheese, peanut butter, brown breadcrumbs, chopped parsley, lemon juice and Marmite. Season to taste with salt and pepper and mix well together. Use an ice-cream scoop to scoop out balls of mixture. Flatten each ball and dip in beaten egg and fresh breadcrumbs. If possible, allow to rest for a couple of hours in the refrigerator before cooking.

Heat the oil and shallow fry the croquettes for 5 minutes on both sides. Drain on kitchen paper and serve, hot and crunchy, with Spicy Tomato Sauce (p.14) and a green salad.

Welsh Lamb and Leek Casserole

2oz/50g butter
1lb/450g neck of lamb, cut into
 large dice
1lb/450g leeks, washed and
 chopped
1 eating apple, peeled, cored
 and sliced
2 tablespoons flour
1 teaspoon mixed herbs or
 1 dessertspoon fresh mixed
 herbs, finely chopped
1 pint/500ml vegetable stock
Salt and pepper to taste
Chopped parsley

Preheat oven to 180°C, 350°F, gas mark 4. Melt a quarter or so of the butter in a frying-pan. Brown the lamb and transfer to a large casserole. Add the leeks and apple slices to the same pan, fry gently for 5 minutes and add to the lamb. Melt the remaining butter in the pan, stir in the flour and cook gently for 2 minutes or so. Add the herbs and stock. Heat gently, stirring all the time until the sauce thickens. Season to taste, then pour over the lamb. Cover and cook for approx. 2 hours until the lamb is tender. Sprinkle with chopped parsley and serve with potatoes or rice. It does not need further vegetables.

Honey Baked Sausages

1lb/450g small sausages
1 tablespoon clear honey
½ tablespoon English mustard
½ tablespoon wholegrain
 mustard

Preheat oven to 180°C, 350F, gas mark 4. Line a baking tin with baking paper. Put the sausages in the tin and spread the honey and mustard to coat them evenly. Bake for about 30 minutes. Serve warm if possible. Sweet Onion Salad (overleaf) is an excellent accompaniment.

Sweet Onion Salad

1 lb/450 g button onions
¼ pint/150 ml red wine
3 fl oz/80 ml olive oil
3 level tablespoons tomato
    purée
1 bay leaf
3 level tablespoons soft light
    brown sugar
Salt and pepper

Peel the onions. The easiest way to do this is to steep them in boiling water for 2 or 3 minutes first. Then put them in a saucepan with all the remaining ingredients, season with salt and pepper and simmer for 20 minutes, or until the onions are tender but still retain their shape. Stir occasionally to prevent the sugar from burning the pan. Cool and transfer the onions and sauce to a bowl. Chill for 10 to 15 minutes before serving. They will keep for several days in a refrigerator.

An excellent salad or relish to serve on a buffet with cold meats. At Erddig, it is often an accompaniment to Honey Baked Sausages (previous page).

Welsh Goats' Cheese Flan

8 oz/225 g shortcrust pastry
2 oz/50 g butter or margarine
1 medium onion, peeled and
    chopped
8 oz/225 g grated goats' cheese
½ pint/250 ml milk or cream
3 eggs
2 tablespoons chopped fresh
    herbs
Salt, pepper and a pinch of
    nutmeg

Preheat oven to 220°C, 425°F, gas mark 7. Roll out the pastry and line a 9 in/23 cm flan tin. Melt the butter or margarine and sauté the onion until soft and golden. Spread over the pastry. Cover with the cheese. Beat the eggs with the milk, add salt, pepper and nutmeg to taste. Pour over the cheese and onion. Sprinkle with fresh herbs: a mixture of parsley, tarragon, and marjoram goes well with the cheese. Bake for 15 minutes, then reduce the temperature to 190°C, 375°F, gas mark 5 and cook for a further 30 minutes.

The cheese used at Erddig is Merlin, a hard goats' cheese from Abergavenny, but any hard goats' cheese will do. Since the cheeses are often salty, watch out when seasoning – the flan may require either no salt or very little.

Watercress, Red Pepper and Nut Loaf

Knob of butter
1 oz/25 g brown breadcrumbs or
ground almonds

LOAF MIXTURE
2 tablespoons olive oil
1 medium onion, peeled and
chopped
8 oz/225 g pine nuts, finely
chopped
4 tablespoons milk
4 oz/125 g fresh white
breadcrumbs
2 eggs
Freshly grated nutmeg, salt and
pepper to taste

STUFFING
1 bunch watercress
1 red pepper, grilled and
skinned
2 tablespoons fresh parsley,
finely chopped
6 oz/175 g fresh brown
breadcrumbs
6 tablespoons olive oil
Juice and finely grated zest of
½ lemon
Salt and pepper to taste

Preheat oven to 190°C, 375°F, gas mark 5. Grease a 2 lb/900 g loaf tin with butter and coat with breadcrumbs or ground almonds.

Heat 2 teaspoons olive oil and sauté the chopped onion gently until soft. Stir in pine nuts, milk, breadcrumbs and eggs to make up the loaf mixture. Add nutmeg, salt and pepper to taste.

For the stuffing, finely chop the watercress and pepper. Combine with parsley, crumbs, olive oil, lemon juice and zest and season to taste with pepper and salt.

Put about two-thirds of the loaf mixture in the prepared tin and press down well to cover the base evenly. Place stuffing on top. Cover with the remaining third of loaf mixture. Cover with foil and bake for approx. an hour.

Inspired by Sophie Grigson, this is on Erddig's Christmas Lunch menu as a colourful and tasty alternative main course for non-meat eaters.

Bara Brith

8oz/225g sultanas or mixed
　　dried fruit
6fl oz/175ml cold Earl Grey tea
8oz/225g wholemeal flour
2oz/50g baking powder
1 teaspoon mixed spice
6oz/175g demerara sugar
Pinch salt
2 eggs, well beaten

Preheat oven to 180°C, 350°F, gas mark 4. Soak the fruit in the cold tea for 5 hours or overnight. Grease and line a 2lb/900g loaf tin. Sift together wholemeal flour and the baking powder, and add spices, sugar and fruit. Mix well. Stir in the eggs. Spoon the mixture into the tin and bake for approx. an hour. Leave to cool in the tin. Keeps well, indeed it even improves.

Bara Brith means 'speckled bread'. Recipes for it are traditional in all Celtic communities.

Iced Carrot and Banana Cake

12oz/350g self-raising flour
1½ teaspoons baking powder
8oz/225g soft light brown sugar
2 bananas, mashed
9oz/250g carrots, grated
4 eggs, well beaten
8fl oz/225ml sunflower oil

BUTTER ICING
2oz/50g unsalted butter
4oz/125g icing sugar
Juice and rind of ½ a lemon

Preheat oven to 180°C, 350°F, gas mark 4. Either grease and flour or line with baking paper a 9in/23cm springform cake tin. Sift flour and baking powder into a mixing bowl which is large enough to hold all the ingredients. Stir in the sugar, bananas, carrots and eggs. Finally stir in the oil. Beat well with a wooden spoon for 5 minutes. Pour into the tin and bake for approx. 45 minutes. Remove from tin and cool on a wire tray.

Ice when cold with the butter icing: soften the butter and beat the sifted sugar into it. Beat in the lemon juice and rind. Spread on the top of the cake, using a fork to make it stand up in peaks.

Erddig Apple Scones

1lb/450g self-raising flour
1 teaspoon salt
4oz/125g butter or margarine
2oz/50g caster sugar
1lb/450g dessert apples
Milk to mix

Preheat oven to 200°C, 400°F, gas mark 6. Grease and flour a baking sheet. Sieve the flour and salt into a large bowl. Add the butter or margarine cut into small pieces and rub into the flour until the mixture resembles coarse breadcrumbs. Stir in caster sugar. Peel and core the apples, grate half and roughly chop the rest. Stir into the mixture. Add sufficient milk to make a soft dough. Turn it on to a floured board. Knead for a couple of minutes, then either cut into 12 or form into two rounds. If you choose rounds, then score each into 6 wedges. Brush the tops with milk, sprinkle with a little sugar and bake for approx. 20 minutes.

At Erddig, apple scones are served with Welsh cheese. Each year the estate holds an Apple Day. The head gardener puts on a display of the old species of apples grown in the garden. There is a demonstration of cider-making by one of the Bulmer cider family, and CAMRC 'real cider' is available to drink. You can buy apples direct from the growers and original pictures of apples direct from the artist. If you are thinking of trying Ellen Jefferies' apple jellies (see pp.50-1), a visit is a 'must'.

Chocolate Chip Cookies

3oz/75g butter or margarine
3oz/75g soft brown sugar
1 egg
Few drops vanilla essence
5oz/150g self-raising flour
Pinch of salt
4oz/125g chocolate chips

Preheat oven to 180°C, 350°F, gas mark 4. Cream the butter or margarine and sugar together until pale and fluffy. Beat in the egg and vanilla essence. Fold in flour, salt and chocolate chips.

Place in teaspoonfuls well apart on a greased baking tray. Bake 10 to 15 minutes, until golden brown. Cool on a wire rack. These biscuits keep well in a tin – if you can stop everyone eating them immediately.

Fruit Jelly Preserves

Ellen Jefferies is famous at Erddig for her spiced jelly preserves using fruits from the garden, orchard and hedgerow and either fresh herbs or spices from the store cupboard. Here are her tips, as she wrote them down, on making these delicious and rewarding delicacies, together with a basic recipe and suggestions for good combinations of flavours. Her crabapple and rosemary recipe produces a pale pink aromatic jelly which both looks and tastes wonderful.

'The principle of jelly making is always the same. Fruit roughly chopped (with peel on where applicable), with spices and/or herbs and lemon rind and juice added, is just covered with water. It is simmered until the fruit is really soft, then strained overnight. The next day the juice obtained is boiled with 1 lb/450g of sugar added to every pint of juice until setting point is reached. An added knob of butter just before skimming helps to disperse the froth. One or two drops of green, yellow or red colouring can then be added if appropriate, as can pectin if it is difficult to obtain a set.

Varieties I have tried quite successfully at different times:

crabapple with thyme; medlar, redcurrant or apple with spices (cinnamon, nutmeg, cloves, etc.); mulberry; blackberry and apple; elderberry and apple; damson and apple; plum and apple; rose petal jelly, with 2oz/50g dark red rose petals, highly scented if possible, added to 2 lb/450g cooking apples.

Any combination can be tried, whatever takes one's fancy!'

APPLE AND SAGE JELLY

2 lb/900 g cooking apples, chopped but not cored or peeled
Large bunch of fresh sage
Pared rind and juice of one lemon
Sugar, granulated or preserving

This recipe takes two days.

Put the apples, sage, lemon rind and juice in a preserving pan. Add sufficient water to cover them. Cover the pan and simmer until the fruit is very soft. This should take about 30 minutes. Strain through a jellybag overnight.

The next day, measure the juice in pints or metric equivalent into a clean preserving pan. Add 1 lb/450 g sugar for each pint of juice. Heat gently until the sugar has dissolved, then boil rapidly until setting point is reached, stirring from time to time. Skim, pour jelly into warm jars and cover. Seal when still hot.

PEAR AND ROSEMARY JELLY

2 lb/900 g pears
Pared rind and juice of 2 lemons
Large bunch of rosemary
Sugar, granulated or preserving
8 fl oz/225 ml pectin, if necessary

Proceed as for Apple and Sage Jelly, adding the pectin at the end if it is difficult to get the jelly to set.

Chocolate Truffles

6 oz/175 g plain chocolate
2 tablespoons brandy or rum (optional)
2 oz/50 g unsalted butter
2 oz/50 g icing sugar
2 oz/50 g ground almonds
Chocolate vermicelli or cocoa

Melt the chocolate in a basin, stir in the brandy or rum, add the butter and stir until melted. Add icing sugar and ground almonds. Cover the bowl and chill until firm. Divide into small balls, roll in vermicelli or cocoa and store covered in the fridge. They keep well for several days. Grated orange rind or coffee essence can be substituted for the brandy or rum, if preferred.

Easy to make, wickedly indulgent; to my taste, home-made truffles are on a different plane from those you can buy ready made.

FLATFORD MILL
SUFFOLK

'But I should paint my own places best . . . I associate my careless boyhood to all that lies on the banks of the Stour. They made me a painter.' John Constable, 1776-1837.

Flatford Mill lies at the heart of what, from his lifetime onwards, has been called 'Constable Country'; a landscape of big skies, water and fields where the inhabitants of this world go about their daily lives, growing crops, fishing and boatbuilding. Throughout John Constable's long battle for recognition from the artistic establishment, he never forgot where his roots lay. Although he painted portraits and other landscapes, he returned throughout his life to these few miles on the borders of Suffolk and Essex for inspiration for some of his greatest paintings.

'We found that the scenery of eight or ten of our late friend's most important subjects might be enclosed by a circle of a few hundred yards at Flatford . . . . So startling was the resemblance of some of these scenes to the pictures of them, which we knew so well, that we could hardly believe we were for the first time standing on the ground from which they were painted.' Charles Leslie, Constable's friend and fellow painter, wrote this in 1843. Our privilege is that, 150 years later, we can still echo Leslie's experience. 'Within this space are the lock which forms the subject of several pictures – Willy Lott's House – the little raised wooden bridge and the picturesque cottage near it . . . and the meadow in which the picture of Boatbuilding was entirely painted.' These subjects are all still recognisable, particularly under the tutelage of the knowledgeable guides who will walk you to the exact spot from which *The Haywain* or *The White Horse* was painted.

Appropriately, apart from the small but fascinating exhibition on Constable's life and career in Bridge Cottage, a visit to Flatford is an entirely outdoor experience. After you have strolled the waterside paths and fields which inspired the painter, visit the tea-garden. It borders the dry dock where the barge in *Boatbuilding* is under construction. Built of wood, the eating area is mainly covered but has no walls. Fronting it is the sleepy River Stour which is no longer fully navigable but where you may hire a rowing boat. Here you can eat lunch and tea, surrounded by flowers, hedgerow birds and squirrels who may want to share your crumbs.

Several of the recipes given here have been served at candlelit suppers where the menus have had a historic theme. They have proved very popular – I am not surprised, the combination of Constable country and good food on a warm summer night must be magical.

Pease Pottage

1lb/450g frozen peas
4oz/125g butter
1 tablespoon fresh mint
Salt, pepper and sugar
Swirl of cream

Defrost the peas and put them in a saucepan with the butter. Put the lid on and cook very slowly until they become mushy. This will take up to 45 minutes. Season with salt, pepper and a teaspoon of sugar and stir in the fresh mint chopped very fine. Serve with a swirl of cream.

In the Middle Ages, 'pottage', a semi-liquid dish eaten with a spoon, was consumed by everyone. Vegetable pottages like this were for the poor; the rich enjoyed spicy meat or fish pottages. At Flatford it is served as a 'winter warmer' at candlelit suppers. It also makes an excellent vegetable accompaniment to the Baked Gammon on p.78.

Scotch Collops with Forcemeat Balls

COLLOPS

1 lb/450g veal escalope
2 oz/50g butter
1 oz/25g flour
½ pint/250 ml beef stock
1 glass white wine
1 teaspoon chopped fresh thyme
Thinly cut peel of 1 orange
Shredded rind of ½ lemon

FORCEMEAT BALLS

7 oz/205 g fresh white
 breadcrumbs
2 oz/50 g shredded suet
2 oz/50 g lean bacon
1 tablespoon parsley, chopped
1 tablespoon fresh thyme,
 chopped
Grated rind of ½ lemon
1 egg, beaten
Salt and pepper to taste
1 oz/25 g butter for frying

Warm a large serving dish in the oven while you are preparing this dish.

Cut the veal into strips ¼ in/6 mm thick and approx. 5 in × 2 in/13 cm × 5 cm. Melt the butter in a large frying-pan and fry the collops a few minutes on each side until evenly brown. Transfer to a large shallow saucepan or sauté pan. Stir the flour into the frying-pan juices and cook for a few seconds, then add stock together with wine, thyme and orange peel. Bring to the boil so it just thickens a little, and pour over the collops.

Now prepare the forcemeat balls. Mix together breadcrumbs, suet, bacon, parsley and thyme, lemon rind and seasoning. Stir in the beaten egg and form into small balls about 1½ in/4 cm in diameter. Melt the butter in a frying-pan and fry the forcemeat balls until brown. Add to the collops and sauce. Cover and simmer gently for about 10 minutes.

Transfer to the warmed serving dish. Extract and discard the orange peel and garnish with shredded lemon peel.

This dish is a modern adaptation of late seventeenth-century recipes from Sara Paston-Williams's *The Art of Dining*. It was served very successfully at one of the Georgian evenings at Flatford.

Suffolk Country Crumble

1 lb/450 g cooked gammon or bacon, cut into thick strips
3 oz/75 g butter
1½ oz/40 g plain flour
1 tablespoon mustard powder
½ pint/250 ml creamy milk
½ pint/250 ml ham or vegetable stock
4 oz/250 g mature Cheddar, finely grated
6 oz/175 g button mushrooms

TOPPING
2 oz/50 g porridge oats
2 oz/50 g hazelnuts, chopped
2 oz/50 g breadcrumbs

Preheat oven to 180°C, 350°F, gas mark 4. Lay strips of ham in the bottom of an ovenproof dish. Make a thick sauce using two-thirds of the butter and all the flour, mustard powder, milk and stock. Add the cheese, taste and add salt and pepper as you wish. Cook the mushrooms gently for 5 minutes in the remaining butter and add with their juices to the sauce. Pour the sauce over the ham. Mix oats, hazelnuts and breadcrumbs together and spread thickly over the top so the sauce does not show at all. Reheat for 20 minutes in the oven and, if necessary, put under a hot grill for a minute or two to ensure that the top is crisp. Serve with a green salad.

Potato Pudding

6 oz/175 g savoury shortcrust pastry
1 tablespoon brandy
¼ pint/150 ml single cream
2 eggs
½ teaspoon cinnamon
1 lb/450 g potatoes (preferably Desirée) cooked, peeled and diced
1 oz/25 g butter, cut into dice
Salt and pepper to taste

Preheat oven to 180°C, 350°F, gas mark 4. Line a 9 in/23 cm flan dish with pastry and bake blind for approx. 15 minutes. Beat the brandy, cream, eggs and cinnamon together for a minute or two. Stir in the diced potato, mix well and fill the flan case with the mixture. Dot the top with the butter and put back into the oven for approx. 30 minutes, until the top is nicely brown.

This too is an adaptation from a historic recipe in *The Art of Dining*. It was served with a Râgout of Cucumber, also from *The Art of Dining*, which at Flatford was cooked in a microwave – a nice combination of old flavours and modern technology.

Apricot, Honey and Rosemary Mousse

2oz/50g butter
1lb/450g semi-dried apricots
Water
3oz/75g honey
2 sprigs fresh rosemary
1 tablespoon gelatine
½ pint/250ml double cream

Melt the butter in a saucepan, add the apricots and turn in the butter. Add water just to cover the fruit, bring to the boil, reduce the heat, simmer until tender, then purée. Heat the honey so it can be measured in a measuring jug, and add to purée. Add the rosemary and leave in the purée to infuse while it cools.

When the purée is completely cold, remove the rosemary. Melt the gelatine in a little hot water and stir into the purée. Whip the cream and fold into the purée. Pile into glasses and garnish with a tiny sprig of rosemary and a little chopped apricot.

Almond, Orange and Lemon Tart

6oz/175g shortcrust pastry
15fl oz/450ml whipping cream
3oz/75g caster or granulated
    sugar
3oz/75g ground almonds
¼ teaspoon almond essence
¼ teaspoon orange flower water
1 tablespoon candied peel
3 large egg whites
2 small lemons
2 small oranges

Preheat oven to 160°C, 325°F, gas mark 3. Roll out and line a 10in/25cm deep flan dish with shortcrust pastry. Bring the cream up to the boil with a slice of lemon peel. Take off the heat and allow to cool. In a bowl large enough to take all the ingredients, mix the sugar, almonds, flavourings and candied peel. Whisk the egg whites until stiff and gently fold into the cooled cream, then fold the egg whites and cream into the rest of the ingredients. Pour into the pastry case. Slice the oranges and lemons thinly and cover the whole of the top of the flan with the slices. Scatter the top with a little extra sugar and bake for an hour. Serve warm or cold.

This has a subtle, unusual flavour. It is an adaptation of an old recipe from a domestic diary kept by Mrs Marguerite Ackworth, and was served as part of a Georgian candlelit supper at Flatford.

Chocolate Fudge Cake

8 oz/225 g caster sugar
8 oz/225 g margarine
2 eggs
9 oz/250 g self-raising flour
4 tablespoons/60 g cocoa
2 teaspoons bicarbonate of soda
12 fl oz/360 ml milk

Preheat oven to 180°C, 350°F, gas mark 4. Line a 9 in/21 cm springform tin with baking paper. Either melt the sugar and margarine together in the microwave or on the top of the stove in a small saucepan. Transfer to a bowl large enough to take all the ingredients. Allow the sugar mixture to cool, then beat the eggs and stir into the mixture. Sift the flour and cocoa together and mix the bicarbonate of soda with the milk, then fold both gently into the mixture. Pour into the tin and bake for up to an hour, or until a skewer comes clean out of the centre. Cool for 10 minutes in the tin, then on a wire tray.

To ice the cake, use the recipe from Souter Lighthouse on p.122. This delicious cake even improves with age.

Milk Punch

4 large lemons
1 pint/500 ml brandy
1 pint/500 ml still mineral water
12 oz/350 g granulated sugar
1 pint/500 ml milk

Grate the zest from lemons into a large bowl. Squeeze juice from lemons and reserve. Pour brandy over the lemon zest and leave for 2 to 3 hours. Then strain the mixture and add lemon juice, sugar and mineral water. Stir well. Bring the milk to the boil and pour into the mixture which will immediately curdle. Cover and leave the bowl overnight.

The next morning strain the mixture through a jelly bag. The liquid will run clear. Reheat to just below boiling and, if possible, serve in small glasses ladled from a punch bowl.

This lethally delicious concoction is based on a Georgian recipe. It makes an unusual drink and guarantees any party will go with a swing.

FLORENCE COURT
CO. FERMANAGH

In her autobiography, *Astride the Wall*, Ursula Wyndham wrote 'Florence Court was one of the most beautiful and magnificently executed of any Palladian house I have ever seen.' Praise indeed from a lady who should know – Ursula Wyndham was brought up in the magnificent Petworth House in Sussex.

An elegant grey mansion, Florence Court is set in landscaped parkland in Co. Fermanagh, the most westerly province of Ulster. It was built in the late eighteenth century by John Cole, 1st Earl of Enniskillen. The Coles were an Anglo-Irish Protestant family with a long local association with the small town of Enniskillen, which is about eight miles away. The state rooms on the ground floor are dignified and formal; fine plasterwork has been restored following a disastrous fire in 1955.

A collection of handsome eighteenth-century Irish furniture is subtly different from English pieces of the same period. The basement is empty, but the maze of rooms provides an interesting glimpse into the world of the servants who ran the Cole household until after the Second World War.

Their lives cannot have been easy when the young Ursula stayed at Florence Court during the 1930s. Her uncle, the 5th Earl of Enniskillen, was head of the family. At breakfast, 'we children were ranged around the walls of the room and forbidden to fidget or speak. . . . Lord Enniskillen was fond of finding fault and his wife had the responsibility of bringing to the cook's notice anything that failed to please. Ten to one the cook then left. The master of the house would throw the toast across the room, fulminating that it was dry. As it had been carried a great distance along stone passages from the subterranean kitchen, this was a frequent occurrence.'

After assessing for myself the impossibility of providing hot toast I wonder how many cooks came and went during the 5th Earl's regime. Simple lunches and teas are now to be had in the Old Kitchen in the North Wing – not the subterranean chamber of Ursula's memory.

Wheaten Bread

8 oz/225 g *wholemeal flour*
8 oz/225 g *strong white flour*
1 teaspoon *baking powder*
4 oz/125 g *margarine*
4 oz/125 g *sugar*
1 egg, *beaten*
12 fl oz/360 ml *buttermilk*

Preheat oven to 200°C, 400°F, gas mark 6. Grease either 2 × 1 lb/2 × 450g loaf tins or 1 × 2 lb/1 × 900g loaf tin.

Sift together all the dry ingredients except the sugar. Rub in the margarine until the mixture resembles coarse breadcrumbs. Add the sugar and stir well. Make a well in the centre and gradually work in the buttermilk and egg until you have a soft dough. Knead lightly. Form into one large loaf or two smaller ones. Place in the tins, brush with milk and bake until well risen and golden brown. The tin should sound hollow when knocked and a skewer should come out of the loaf clean. For a 2 lb/900g loaf this may take 1¼ hours, but the smaller loaves need a little less time; have a look at them after ¾ hour.

In Ireland, breadmaking as well as sconemaking is highly esteemed. Wheaten bread warm from the oven and spread with Ulster butter is irresistible!

Boiled Fruit Cake

4oz/125g butter or margarine
8oz/225g soft brown sugar
Small tin of crushed pineapple
  (approx. 7½oz/213g)
4oz/125g glacé cherries, cut in
  half
1lb/450g mixed dried fruit
12oz/350g self-raising flour
1 tablespoon mixed spice
3 eggs, well beaten

Preheat oven to 150°C, 300°F, gas mark 2. Line an 8in/20cm loose-bottomed cake tin with baking paper. Put butter or margarine, sugar, pineapple, cherries and dried fruit in a saucepan. Bring to the boil, boil for a couple of minutes, then turn off the heat and leave to cool. When cool, transfer to large mixing bowl and stir in the flour and mixed spice sifted together. Add the beaten eggs, mix well and transfer to the cake tin. Bake for approx. 2 hours, or until a steel skewer comes out clean from the centre of the cake.

This is a moist, light version of an old favourite. It keeps well and can improve with age – if not eaten!

Treacle Cake

1lb/450g plain flour
1 tablespoon mixed spice
4oz/125g butter
8oz/225g mixed dried fruit
2oz/50g glacé cherries, cut in
  half
6oz/175g soft brown sugar
3 tablespoons treacle
3 tablespoons hot water
3 eggs

Preheat oven to 150°C, 300°F, gas mark 2. Line a 9in/23cm cake tin with baking paper. Sift the flour with the mixed spice into a bowl large enough to take all the ingredients. Rub the butter into the flour until the mixture resembles fine crumbs. Stir in the dried fruit and most of the cherries (keep a few to decorate the top of the cake). Stir in the sugar and make a well in the centre of the cake. Mix the treacle with the hot water. Beat the eggs well and add the treacle mixture and the beaten eggs alternately until the cake mixture drops from the spoon. Place in the tin and decorate the top with the remaining cherries. Bake on the middle shelf of the oven for an hour, or until a skewer comes out clean. Cool in the tin.

This is an old recipe. It produces a dark, moist cake which keeps well.

FOUNTAINS ABBEY
YORKSHIRE

The size, beauty and setting of Fountains Abbey take the breath away. Even in ruins, it is easy to comprehend that this was a place of power and influence. How did this happen? And why, eventually, did it fail?

Fountains Abbey, founded in 1132, was a Cistercian monastery. Austerity and simplicity are the hallmarks of the Cistercian way of life. The same values hold good in their architecture, a severe unadorned style relying for impact on mass and proportion, light and shade. The buildings, like the monks' lives, were dedicated to the glory of God. Careful planning allowed the monks to devote as much time as possible to their vocation: prayer leading to a mystical communion with God.

'Choir' monks lived lives of rigorous simplicity. Each day began with prayers at 2.30am. Seven services punctuated long periods of silence when communication was only by gesture. The monks were forbidden to have underwear and wore coarse undyed habits of sheeps' wool. Their diet was barely above subsistence level, only the sick were allowed to eat 'meat of quadrupeds'. The monks would never have been able to devote so much time to meditation and contemplation if it had not been for the lay brothers, a very different community of men who were the Abbey's labour force.

Unlike the choir monks, the lay brothers were mostly illiterate. They took monastic vows and shared the church, but lived separate lives (hence the enormous size of the Abbey complex). They attended fewer services, slept longer, ate more food and served the community as masons, tanners and shoemakers or brewers and bakers. However, their most important role was as 'shepherds for God', looking after the Abbey's vast flocks of sheep which grazed estates far from Fountains. By the thirteenth century this was one of the richest religious houses in England.

Wealth and idealism do not mix. Encouraged by the presence of the lay brothers, the monks overextended themselves. Control was lost, economic collapse followed. The Abbot of Fountains retained his seat in Parliament until Henry VIII dissolved the monasteries in the 1530s, but their power had gone, never to return.

The restaurant at the Visitors' Centre, which serves both the Abbey and John Aislabie's wonderful water garden at Studley Royal, is modern, spacious and even larger than the refectory in the original Abbey. It seems entirely appropriate that, like the monk's diet, the recipes which they have given me do not include 'the flesh of quadrupeds'.

Salmon and Sour Cream Pie

COURT BOUILLON
¼ pint/150 ml lemon juice or
  white wine made up to
  ¾ pint/400 ml with water
A few peppercorns
2 garlic cloves
A little celery, finely chopped
  parsley stalks

PIE
12 oz/350 g salmon fillet,
  allowing 3 oz/75 g per person
3 eggs, hardboiled
A large handful of finely
  chopped parsley
Half cream
2 oz/50 g butter
1 tablespoon plain flour
8 oz/225 g puff pastry
Egg wash to glaze the pastry

Preheat oven to 220°C, 425°F, gas mark 7. Combine all the court bouillon ingredients in a saucepan and bring to the boil. Reduce the heat and poach the salmon for 10 minutes in the bouillon. Leave it to cool in the liquid.

In a pie dish, quarter the eggs and divide the salmon into chunks, discarding any bones. Scatter the parsley over the top. Strain the fish stock, make it up to 1 pint/500 ml with the cream or milk. Melt the butter, stir in the flour, cook for 5 minutes very gently and make a creamy sauce with the stock mixture. Pour this over the salmon and eggs. Leave to cool before covering with puff pastry. Glaze and cook for 20 minutes until the pastry is golden.

The fish stock 'sours' the cream for the sauce.

Fish and Cider Casserole

1½ lb/675 g coley fillets
½ pint/250 ml vegetable stock
1 onion, peeled and sliced
2 oz/50 g butter
2 oz/50 g plain flour
½ pint/250 ml cider
2 teaspoons anchovy essence
1 tablespoon lemon juice
Salt and pepper to taste

TOPPING
8 oz/225 g peeled and sliced
  cooked potatoes
8 oz/225 g peeled and sliced
  apples
1 oz/25 g butter

Preheat oven to 150°C, 300°F, gas mark 2. Poach coley in stock until cooked, approx. 10 minutes. Set aside while you make the sauce. Sauté the onion in butter until cooked but not coloured. Stir in the flour and cook gently for a further 5 minutes. Stir in the cider, anchovy essence and lemon juice. Then use as much of the stock as you wish to make the sauce thick, but not too thick. Divide the coley fillets into six portions and place in a gratin dish. Pour over the cider sauce, coating the fish evenly. Cover with foil and place it in the oven to keep warm while you prepare the topping.

At this point, preheat grill. Melt the extra ounce (25 g) of butter in a frying-pan and gently fry the cooked potato and the apple slices for a few minutes. Arrange them on the top of the dish to cover the fish mixture completely. Then pop the dish under the grill for 5 minutes to brown the top before serving.

THE GIANT'S CAUSEWAY
CO. ANTRIM

Are you a romantic? If you are, the Giant's Causeway was built by the legendary Irish giant, Finn McCool, to get to Scotland to fight his rival, Benandonner. But perhaps you seek scientific explanations? If so, the 40,000 amazingly precise columns of dark basalt composing the Causeway were formed as a result of the even cooling of volcanic lava 55 million years ago.

The Causeway is only part of the geological and natural marvels waiting for scientists and romantics and indeed anyone who visits the wild and beautiful north Antrim coast. It lies in the middle of a great green amphitheatre, an apt setting for such dramatic rock formations as the Harp, the Chimney Tops and the Organ, as well as the Causeway basalts which march into the sea to emerge 50 miles away on the other side of the Irish Sea as the basalt stacks of Staffa and Fingal's Cave. Birdwatchers are in paradise. Overhead soar guillemots, razorbills, oystercatchers and fulmar petrels. Deep blue harebells and pink thrift catch the eye. More serious botanists can find wonderful plants: sea spleenwort, vernal squill, sea fescue and frog orchard all flourish here. The air is strong, clean and clear. The day I visited, within the space of an hour, we had rain and sun and the sea colour varied from dark, forbidding grey/green to deep cobalt blue.

Travellers have been intrigued by the Causeway for centuries. In the Visitors' Centre there are photographs of intrepid Victorian ladies in crinolines clambering on the columns. Today, visitors come from all over the world. Stout shoes are the order of the day for walkers. The infirm, or less energetic, can ride down on a minibus.

Either way, after marvelling at nature, or Finn McCool, call in on the light, bright restaurant. Looking out over the cliffs and sea you can warm up with soups that are a meal in themselves, treat yourself to a salmon salad, or reward yourself with one of the home-baked cakes or biscuits that Northern Irish cooks are famous for.

Leek and Potato Soup

1 pint/500ml vegetable stock
1lb/450g leeks, cleaned and chopped
1½lb/675g potatoes, peeled and diced
2oz/50g butter
2 tablespoons flour
1 pint/500ml creamy milk

Heat the vegetable stock in a pan large enough to take all the ingredients, put in the leeks and potatoes, bring to the boil and simmer until the vegetables are tender. Meanwhile melt the butter in a small pan, stir in the flour and cook very gently for 5 minutes until it is a biscuit colour. Add the milk, stirring continuously to make a thick, creamy béchamel. When the leeks and potatoes are cooked, combine the two and season to taste. It should need very little salt, but freshly ground black pepper brings out the flavours beautifully.

Carrot and Lentil Soup

2 tablespoons sunflower oil
1 medium onion, finely chopped
8 oz/225 g red lentils
2 pints/1250 ml vegetable stock
2 carrots weighing approx. 8 oz/
225 g, finely grated

GARNISH (optional)
Chopped parsley or coriander
A little single cream

Heat the sunflower oil in a large saucepan and sauté the onion for a few minutes, add the lentils and turn them in the oil for 5 minutes. Pour in the vegetable stock, bring the mixture to the boil and then simmer until the lentils and onion are soft, approx. 15 minutes. Liquidise the lentil mixture, add the grated carrot and return the soup to the pan. Add salt and pepper to taste. Reheat the soup and simmer for 5 minutes, stirring to stop it sticking.

Serve piping hot, with a swirl of cream and a little chopped coriander or parsley if you wish.

Irish Stew

1 tablespoon vegetable oil
1 lb/450 g neck fillet of lamb cut
    into chunks
1 large onion, sliced
2 medium carrots, peeled and
    cut into short lengths
1 stick of celery (optional),
    chopped
12 oz/350 g new potatoes,
    scrubbed
Approx. 1¼ pints/¾ litre
    vegetable stock
8 oz/225 g cooked potato,
    mashed
Salt and pepper to taste

Preheat oven to 150°C, 300°F, gas mark 2. Heat the oil in a cast-iron casserole and fry the meat and the onions together until nicely browned. Take the casserole off the heat and add the carrots, the celery and the potatoes. Stir and add the vegetable stock to cover the meat and vegetables. Bring the casserole to the boil and then either simmer very slowly on the top of the cooker or stew gently in the oven until the meat is tender and the vegetables are cooked but still have a little crunch. Stir in the mashed potato to thicken the gravy and season to taste with salt and pepper.

This is a delicious traditional dish which makes use of the excellent raw ingredients available in Ulster. It needs no further accompaniment but if you like a piquant relish with it, the recipe for Red Cabbage Pickle on p.145 is perfect.

Beef and Guinness Casserole

1 tablespoon vegetable oil
1lb/450g steak, cubed
8oz/225g onions, chopped
15fl oz/450ml Guinness
8oz/225g carrots, peeled and
    cut into fine matchsticks
A little cornflour to thicken the
    sauce
Salt and pepper to taste

Preheat oven to 150°C, 300°F, gas mark 2. Heat the oil in a cast-iron casserole and fry the steak and the onions until all are nicely browned. Pour over the Guinness – it should cover the meat and the onions, but if it does not, add a little water. Cover the pan and cook in a slow oven until the meat is just tender. At this point add the carrots and cook for a further 30 to 45 minutes. Thicken the gravy with a little cornflour – probably about a tablespoon creamed with a little water. Season with salt and pepper.

This uses two of Ireland's best-known products – beef and stout. Because they are so good and so complimentary to each other there is no need for complex spices or herbs. The recipe is simple, the result delicious. It is good served with Champ (below).

Champ

1½lb/675g potatoes
½ pint/250ml buttermilk
Salt and pepper to taste
6 spring onions, finely chopped
2oz/50g butter

Peel, boil and drain potatoes. Heat the buttermilk gently in a saucepan and mash the potatoes with the buttermilk until they are very smooth. Season with salt and pepper and stir in the chopped spring onions which can either be fresh or blanched for a more delicate flavour. Put a mound of champ on each plate. Make a well in the centre and fill it with a knob of butter. Serve immediately.

This very old Irish recipe is traditionally served as an accompaniment to fish. In the Crown Liquor Saloon in Belfast, also owned by the National Trust, you can have Champ with Oysters – a real treat.

Date Krispies

4oz/125g margarine or butter
8oz/225g sugar
8oz/225g chopped dates
8oz/225g syrup
8oz/225g Rice Krispies
3oz/75g plain chocolate

Line a Swiss roll tin, approx. 12 in × 9 in/30 cm × 23 cm with baking paper. Place margarine or butter, sugar, chopped dates and syrup in a saucepan and boil together until just beginning to change colour and caramelise. Take off the heat, allow to cool a little and stir in the Rice Krispies. Press the mixture into the tin. Allow to cool completely. Melt the chocolate and cover the krispies with a thin layer. Cut into squares to serve.

It seems to be a tradition in Northern Ireland to serve small, very sweet 'tray bakes' with tea or coffee or as party food. I chose this recipe as representative because it reminded me of the chocolate krispies I loved as a child.

Almond and Chocolate Chip Cake

5oz/150g plain flour
2 teaspoons baking powder
6oz/175g soft margarine
6oz/175g caster sugar
4oz/125g ground almonds
3 large eggs
½ teaspoon almond essence
2 tablespoons milk
2oz/50g chocolate chips
1oz/25g flaked almonds

Preheat oven to 160°C, 325°F, gas mark 3. Grease and flour or line a 9in/23cm cake tin with baking paper. Sift the flour and baking powder into a large bowl. Add margarine, sugar, ground almonds, eggs, almond essence and milk. Beat until smooth, then for another minute. Stir in chocolate chips and almonds. Turn the mixture into the prepared tin and bake until golden for approx. 1¼ hours. Cool for 5 minutes in the tin, then turn out to cool completely on a wire tray.

HAM HOUSE
SURREY

Strolling slowly through Ham's formal, opulent rooms, it only requires a little imagination to fill this rich bygone world with the kings and courtiers, wives and mistresses whose portraits still line the walls.

Two faces dominate. Elizabeth Murray, Countess of Dysart, 'a pretty witty lass', inherited Ham in 1655. In the Round Gallery you can see her painted by Peter Lely as a red-haired young beauty. In the Long Gallery you will find her, again painted by Lely, as a mature handsome woman with a black servant, the fashionable accessory of the day.

Back in the Round Gallery is 'Both Ye Graces in one Picture'. Here Elizabeth is accompanied by her second husband, John Maitland, Duke of Lauderdale. His is the other dominant face at Ham. The Duke stares directly at us, seated in a great chair which is almost a throne. He is not a handsome man but he is confident of the air of power and influence he conveys. Elizabeth sits on his left. Her dress is rich silk but it seems slightly dishevelled, as does her hair. Her gaze is not direct, her head is turned towards her husband and her sidelong look under heavy eyelids, together with the disorder of her dress and her coquettish gesture, seem to confirm a contemporary comment on their relationship. 'Lady Dysart had such an ascendant over his affections that neither her age, nor his affairs ... could divert him from marrying her within six week's of his Lady's decease.' Age and court intrigue may have dimmed her beauty but not her power.

Age has not dimmed the power of Ham's beauty either. The Lauderdales spent huge sums of money to bring the house and grounds to the pinnacle of Restoration fashion. Here, we can savour a glimpse into that rich past and enjoy the tranquillity of the gardens on the banks of the Thames, a special privilege so close to London.

Wandering through the garden you will find the Orangery where you can eat both simply and imaginatively. Recipes follow for two unusual soups, Pea, Pear and Watercress, and Cucumber, Cumin and Mint. Old favourites like Rack of Lamb jostle newer combinations of flavours, such as Pine Nut Roast with Spicy Plum Sauce. Elizabeth Dysart would have approved of food with flair like this.

Poached Pear with Camembert Sauce

4 pears
1 tablespoon lemon juice
6 fl oz/175 ml crème fraîche
2 tablespoons double cream
2 oz/50 g ripe Camembert,
   chopped
Salt and a pinch of cayenne
   pepper

GARNISH
Fresh mint leaves

Peel the pears and cut in half. Cut out the cores and poach the pears in water, with lemon juice added, until tender. Blend the crème fraîche, double cream and Camembert until smooth, season with cayenne and salt if necessary. Put two pear halves on each plate, pile the Camembert mixture on top and decorate with fresh mint leaves. Chill until ready to serve.

Pea, Pear and Watercress Soup

1 oz/25 g butter
1 small onion, chopped
8 oz/225 g frozen peas
1 lb/450 g pears, peeled and
    chopped (retain one pear to
    use as garnish)
2 pints/1250 ml chicken stock
2–3 bunches of watercress
Salt and pepper to taste

GARNISH
Single cream
Slices of pear fried in a little
    butter

Melt the butter in a saucepan. Sauté the chopped onion and peas until the onion is soft but not coloured. Add chicken stock and pears. Cook for approx. 15 minutes until the pears are soft. Remove from heat, add the watercress. Blend until smooth, season with salt and pepper to taste and re-heat to just below boiling. Serve with a swirl of cream and a couple of slices of fried pear in each dish.

Cucumber, Cumin and Mint Soup

1 dessertspoon olive oil
1 dessertspoon vegetable oil
1 medium onion, peeled and
    chopped
2 cloves garlic, peeled and
    crushed
1 cucumber, chopped but not
    peeled
½ teaspoon ground cumin
¼ teaspoon ground nutmeg
1 bay leaf
1 tablespoon fresh mint, finely
    chopped
1½ pints/750 ml chicken stock
1 tablespoon lemon juice

GARNISH
Single cream
Fresh mint leaves

Heat the oils together in a saucepan. Sauté the onion and garlic until soft but not coloured. Add chopped cucumber, cumin and nutmeg. Stir well and cook for 5 minutes. Add the bay leaf, mint and chicken stock, bring to the boil and simmer until the cucumber is cooked – about 10 minutes. Remove from heat, add lemon juice and blend until smooth. Season with salt and pepper to taste. Allow to cool and chill until required. Serve with a swirl of cream and a couple of mint leaves to complement the delicate green of the soup.

This has a refreshing, tart flavour. It makes a perfect start to a summer dinner.

Gravadlax

1lb/450g fresh salmon fillet,
  skinned
Coarse grain mustard
1 packet fresh dill (dried dill can
  be used)
Rock salt
Freshly ground pepper
Lemon wedges

Ask the fishmonger for a cut from the thick end of the fillet, and allow approx. 2 oz/50g of salmon per serving. Start this dish three days before you wish to serve it.

Cut a piece of cling film large enough to wrap the salmon in. Scatter rock salt on the cling film. Spread both sides of the salmon first with coarse grain mustard, then with the dill finely chopped, to cover the fish completely. Retain the rest of the dill for the recipe below. Wrap the salmon in the cling film and chill for 3 days, turning from time to time. It is not necessary to unwrap the fish.

To serve, remove the cling film, slice the salmon thinly, garnish with lemon wedges, and serve with brown bread and butter, a little green frisée, and the slightly sweet Dill Mayonnaise (below).

Dill Mayonnaise

2 egg yolks
½ teaspoon Dijon mustard
½ pint/250ml olive oil or
  sunflower oil
2 tablespoons lemon juice
2 tablespoons wine vinegar
Salt and pepper
1 teaspoon caster sugar
Fresh dill

It is important that all the ingredients should be at room temperature to emulsify the eggs and oil.

Put the egg yolks and mustard into a bowl and mix thoroughly. Whisk in the oil drop by drop. (This is easiest with an electric mixer or a food processor, but if you can put up with an aching wrist, it is quite possible by hand.) When you have blended in half the oil, add one tablespoon of lemon juice and one of vinegar. Then whisk in the rest of the oil. Chop the remaining dill (or use a dessertspoon of dried dill), and mix with the sugar, salt and black pepper to taste. Stir into the mayonnaise. Taste, it may be perfect for you, but if you prefer a sharper mayonnaise, add the second tablespoon of lemon and vinegar. If made a day in advance, the dill flavour will intensify.

Pine Nut Roast

ROAST
1½ oz/40g butter
2-3 tablespoons toasted
  breadcrumbs
1 small onion, peeled and
  chopped
2 oz/50g pine nuts
4 oz/125g cashew nuts, finely
  chopped
2 oz/50g ground almonds
4 oz/125g fresh breadcrumbs
4 tablespoons milk
2 eggs, beaten
Salt, black pepper and nutmeg
  to taste
2 tablespoons toasted pine nuts
  for topping

STUFFING
4 oz/125g butter
Grated rind and juice of
  ½ lemon
4 tablespoons finely chopped
  parsley
1 clove garlic, crushed
4 oz/125g fresh brown or white
  breadcrumbs

GARNISH
Lemon slices
Parsley sprigs

Preheat oven to 180°C, 350°F, gas mark 4. Line a 2lb/900g loaf tin with greaseproof paper. Brush with melted butter and coat with the toasted crumbs. Use the remaining butter to fry the onion until soft and lightly browned. Turn into a bowl and add nuts, breadcrumbs, milk and eggs. Season with salt, pepper and nutmeg to taste and stir well to mix all the ingredients. Set aside while you make the stuffing.

Cream the butter until soft and gradually work in the lemon, parsley, garlic and breadcrumbs. Blend thoroughly.

Spoon half the roast into the base of the prepared tin. Cover with stuffing, then with the remaining roast mixture. Top with toasted pine nuts, cover with a piece of buttered foil and bake for 1 hour. Remove foil and return to the oven for 5–10 minutes to brown.

Garnish with lemon slices and parsley stalks and serve hot with Spicy Plum Sauce (below).

Spicy Plum Sauce

1 tablespoon vegetable oil
1-2 garlic cloves, peeled and
  crushed
4 oz/125g onion, peeled and
  chopped
8 oz/225g tin stoned plums
8 fl oz/225ml red wine
4 oz/125g brown sugar
Salt and pepper to taste

Heat the oil in a saucepan and sauté the onion and garlic until soft but not browned. Purée the plums and add to the onion together with the red wine. Bring to the boil, then reduce heat and simmer uncovered for approx. 10 minutes, until the sauce is thick enough to cover the back of a spoon. Stir in the sugar and simmer for a further 5 minutes. Taste and season. Serve with Pine Nut Roast (above).

Leek Roulade with Pear and Stilton Filling

1lb/450g leeks, cleaned and
   chopped
6 eggs, separated
Salt, pepper and nutmeg
Parsley to garnish

FILLING
2 pears
4oz/125g Stilton
6oz/175g fromage frais

Preheat oven to 190°C, 375°F, gas mark 5. Line a 14in × 8in/ 33cm × 23cm Swiss roll tin with baking paper. Cook the leeks in plenty of water for 10 minutes, drain and cool. When cool mix with the egg yolks and season to taste with salt, pepper and nutmeg. Whisk the egg whites until very stiff, fold into the leek mixture. Transfer to the prepared tin and smooth into the corners. Bake for approx. 15 minutes, until brown and firm to the touch. Cool in the tin covered with a damp tea towel while you make up the filling.

Peel the pears and slice thinly. Crumble the Stilton and mix with fromage frais. When the roulade is cool, turn out on to a clean piece of greaseproof paper. Peel off the baking paper and spread with the Stilton mixture. Arrange the pear slices on top and roll up the roulade, using the paper as an aid. Slide on to a serving dish, garnish with parsley and serve at room temperature.

Good as part of a buffet; alternatively, a thick slice surrounded by tomato coulis makes a colourful first course of contrasting flavours.

Mocha Meringue Log

4 egg whites
8oz/225g caster sugar
1 pint/500ml double cream
1 dessertspoon coffee essence
3oz/75g toasted flaked almonds

Preheat oven to 220°C, 425°F, gas mark 7. Line a 14in × 8in/ 23cm × 33cm Swiss roll tin with baking paper. Whisk egg whites until standing up in peaks. Then whisk in the sugar, a teaspoonful at a time. You will have a stiff shiny meringue. Spread the meringue into the prepared tin and bake for 8 minutes. It should be slightly brown. Turn out on to more baking paper and peel off the cooking paper while the roulade is still warm. Cool. Whip the cream with the coffee essence until stiff and use about half to fill the meringue. Roll up the meringue using the paper as an aid. Don't worry if it splits. Spread the rest of the cream over the top of the meringue and cover in toasted almonds. Use the paper to slide on to a serving plate and chill until required.

Delicious served with fresh soft fruit such as raspberries.

KEDLESTON HALL
DERBYSHIRE

Kedleston is one of the grandest houses in England. Unlike many other Trust properties, Kedleston has been 'on view' since the day it was finished. Perhaps this is a reason for the remarkable survival of both the interiors and the exteriors. To all intents and purposes, the first panoramic view of the great mansion, magnificently dominating its own great park, the positioning of the pictures and the furniture in the state rooms, the decorative schemes of those rooms are all exactly as the owner, Nathaniel Curzon, 1st Lord Scarsdale, and Robert Adam, the architect, planned in the 1760s.

Lord Scarsdale and Robert Adam were both in their thirties when Kedleston was being built, and exuberance and arrogance are part of the whole concept. Lord Scarsdale razed an entire village to improve visitors' first view of the house. The furniture in the state rooms is an extraordinary combination of the monumental and the exotic. Golden plumes crown the mirrors while the state bed is a riot of palm trees and fronds.

It never occurred to Adam that any changes would ever be made to his grand design. There are no skirtings behind the wonderful sofas supported by voluptuous tritons and sea-nymphs in the Saloon, and no paint behind Lord Scarsdale's paintings, hung to Adam's plans. Kedleston is a true mirror of eighteenth-century taste in both architecture and the decorative arts.

A later Curzon was to become even more famous than the house itself:

> My name is George Nathaniel Curzon
> I am a most superior person.

At the foot of the Great Staircase, you can see a full-length portrait of George Nathaniel at his most superior, elegantly dressed as Viceroy of India. Opposite is his young American wife, Mary, looking poised and beautiful in the famous Peacock Dress she wore for the Coronation Durbar in India in 1903.

Mary's first visit to Kedleston must have been quite an ordeal. Not only did she meet George Nathaniel's father and his eight younger brothers and sisters for the first time, but she also had to receive a scroll of welcome from the local tenantry. The formality of late Victorian English upper-class life must have been very difficult for a young foreigner from a very different society. Her husband's appointment as Viceroy offered a welcome possibility to make a newer, happier life with the man she loved, but sadly the Indian climate undermined her health. She died, aged 36, less than a year after their return. Curzon wrote sadly 'I owe to her all the happiness of my life', and buried her at Kedleston beneath a magnificent marble monument in All Saints' Church.

The Great Kitchen has 'Waste not, Want not' inscribed over the giant range and spit. Above one end is a gallery supported on fine Doric columns. Like the state rooms, this kitchen has always expected visitors. Now the restaurant, it still does. You can enjoy hearty lunches and good home-made teas served on the four huge, original, scrubbed kitchen tables.

Creamy Fish Soup

1 lb/450 g smoked haddock
  or cod
1 medium onion
1 pint/500 ml full cream milk
1 pint/500 ml fish stock
1 small tin sweetcorn approx.
  8 oz/225 g
8 oz/225 g cooked potato, cubed
Salt and pepper to taste
Paprika and parsley to garnish

Steam or poach the fish for 5 minutes. Remove from the water with a slotted spoon. Discard the skin and any bones. Divide the fish into chunks with a fork. Use the water to make up the fish stock.

Peel and finely chop the onion and place in a large saucepan with the milk and stock. Simmer until tender (about 10 to 15 minutes), then add the potatoes and sweetcorn. Reheat until just below boiling, add the fish and season to taste. Serve immediately, garnishing the soup bowls with a dusting of paprika and a little chopped parsley.

A Kedleston special – more a full meal than a starter.

Lady Curzon's Chicken

1 lb/450 g cooked chicken
2 fresh peaches
Juice of 1 lemon
1 dessertspoon mild curry paste
1 tablespoon either apricot jam
  or mango chutney
4 tablespoons mayonnaise
2 tablespoons Greek yoghurt
Salt and pepper
Peach slices and lettuce leaves as
  garnish

Take the chicken off the bone and cut into chunks manageable with a fork. Peel the peaches and cut into slices. Stir into the lemon juice. (This will stop the slices discolouring if the salad is not being served immediately). In a bowl large enough to take all the ingredients, blend together the curry paste, jam or chutney, mayonnaise and Greek yoghurt. Season to taste with salt and pepper. Stir in the chicken and peach slices.

Line a serving dish with a bed of lettuce, pile up the chicken mayonnaise and garnish with peach slices.

This is a delicious variation on 'Coronation Chicken' and makes an excellent dish for a summer buffet party.

Baked Gammon with Cider and Apple Sauce

4lb/1.8kg piece of gammon
15fl oz/450ml cider
Small quantity of onion, carrot,
    celery for stock
Peppercorns or freshly ground
    pepper
2 teaspoons Dijon mustard
A few whole cloves
2 tablespoons sugar
1oz/25g butter
1 tablespoon chopped onion
1 eating apple
1oz/25g flour

Place the gammon joint in a saucepan. Pour in the cider and add sufficient water to cover, add the onion, carrot and celery plus either a little ground pepper or a few whole peppercorns. Cover the pan and bring the liquid to the boil, reduce the heat and simmer joint for approx. 1 hour.

Strain off and reserve the stock. Turn the oven on to full heat. Place the joint in a roasting pan. Slice off skin leaving a layer of fat on the joint. Smear the fat with the mustard and sugar and score with a sharp knife as if you were laying out a noughts-and-crosses game. Stud the pattern with cloves. Pour in a little of the ham stock to stop the joint sticking and return it to the hot oven. Roast for 15 minutes, then turn off the oven and leave the joint to rest for at least 10 minutes.

In a small saucepan, melt the butter and sauté the onion and apple for approx. 5 minutes. Add the flour, stir well and cook gently for a further 5 minutes. Gradually add the stock until you have a medium thick sauce, then turn the heat well down and simmer until the apple and onion are very soft. When the gammon is ready, stir the juices from the roasting pan into the sauce. Slice the ham thinly, serve the sauce separately. Plain steamed vegetables are a perfect contrast to the rich tangy sauce and the piquant ham.

I have suggested a rather large joint as it is also extremely good served cold. The same recipe works well with a smoked bacon shoulder if you need to economise.

Onion Pie

PASTRY
6 oz/175 g wholemeal flour
4 oz/125 g butter or baking
  margarine
A little cold water

FILLING
1 oz/25 g butter or margarine
1 lb/450 g onions, thinly sliced
8 fl oz/225 g single cream
1 tablespoon lemon juice
1 tablespoon wholemeal flour
3 eggs
Pinch of powdered cloves and
  cayenne pepper
Salt to taste

Preheat oven to 190°C, 375°F, gas mark 5. Rub the butter or baking margarine into the wholemeal flour and add a little cold water to make up the pastry. Roll it out and line a 9 in/ 23 cm pie plate. Chill while you assemble the filling.

Melt the butter or margarine and fry the onions gently until soft (approx. 20 minutes). Beat together the cream, lemon juice, wholemeal flour and eggs and season with cloves, cayenne pepper and salt to taste. Spread the onions evenly over the pastry base. Pour the egg and cream mixture over the onions. *Do not stir.* Bake for 15 minutes, then lower the heat to 160°C, 325°F, gas mark 3 and bake for approx. 15 more minutes, until the pastry is golden and the filling set. Serve warm.

Mushroom and Lentil Pie

MUSHROOM FILLING
1 tablespoon olive oil
1 clove garlic, crushed
1 lb/450 g flat mushrooms,
  chopped finely
2 oz/50 g fresh wholemeal
  breadcrumbs
5 fl oz/125 ml crème fraîche or
  soured cream
1 egg, beaten

LENTIL FILLING
8 oz/225 g red lentils
¾ pint/400 ml water
1 tablespoon vegetable oil
1 medium onion, finely chopped
2 tablespoons tomato purée
3 tablespoons parsley, chopped
1 egg, beaten
Salt and pepper

PIE CRUST
1 lb/450 g shortcrust pastry
Egg and milk wash

Preheat oven to 190°C, 375°F, gas mark 5. To make the mushroom filling, heat the oil and sauté the garlic for 2 minutes. Take off the heat and stir in the mushrooms, breadcrumbs, crème fraîche and egg.

To make the lentil filling put the lentils in a saucepan, cover with the water. Bring to the boil, then reduce the heat and simmer until the water is absorbed. Heat the oil and fry the onions gently until soft. Add to the lentils together with the tomato purée, parsley and egg. Season to taste.

Roll out the pastry and use two-thirds to line an 8 in/ 20 cm springform cake tin. Fill in layers, first the mushroom, then all the lentil mixture, then mushroom. Top with the remaining third of pastry. Use any trimmings to decorate the top of the pie. Glaze with the egg wash. Bake for approx. 1¾ hours. Keep an eye on the pie and cover the top with foil when it is nicely browned.

Served at room temperature, this pie makes a substantial vegetarian main course. It is also excellent for a picnic.

Potted Stilton

10oz/230g Stilton
2oz/50g softened butter
Pinch of mace
Pinch of cayenne pepper
2 tablespoons port or milk
2oz/50g clarified butter

Blend Stilton, softened butter, mace and cayenne together with the port or milk to make a smooth spreadable paste. Pack into small ramekin dishes. Melt the remaining butter and pour over the Stilton to seal the ramekins, taking care to leave behind the milky sediment. Chill until required.

This is an excellent recipe for Christmas Stilton in January, when it is getting a little dry. It keeps well for up to two weeks in a refrigerator.

Chocolate and Orange Delights

8oz/225g plain flour
8oz/225g baking margarine
4oz/125g icing sugar
4oz/125g custard powder
Marmalade (not too chunky)
4oz/125g plain chocolate

Preheat oven to 200°C, 400°F, gas mark 6. Grease and flour or line baking trays with baking paper. Put the flour, margarine, icing sugar and custard powder in the food processor and process until the mixture forms a ball of dough around the blade. Roll out and cut out rounds with a 4in/10cm cutter. Bake for 15 minutes until lightly coloured, turning if necessary. Cool on a wire tray.

When cold spread thinly with marmalade. Melt chocolate and pour over the top to cover. Allow to cool completely so the chocolate is crisp again before serving.

A home-made version of Jaffa cakes. The tartness of the marmalade contrasts very well with the chocolate.

KILLERTON
DEVON

Killerton was built in 1778 by Sir Thomas Dyke Acland as a temporary residence. Now pleasantly permanent, the house is not a show-piece in the accepted sense but a family house that many visitors can imagine living in.

The Aclands can trace their family back to the twelfth century, to Hugh de Accalen, a small freeholder at Acland Barton near Landkey in North Devon. Splendid marriages increased their lands, wealth and influence but they always remained devoted Devonians. Never absentee landlords, they had a deep sense of public duty. Generations of Aclands served as Members of Parliament, Justices of the Peace and Sheriffs.

The ground-floor rooms are furnished as they would have been in the 1930s when

Sir Francis, his wife Eleanor, and their family lived here. Fresh flowers, photographs and memorabilia rub shoulders with antiques and family portraits. It is probably quieter and tidier now than then; the house was always full of people, four lively children, pet dogs and friends mixed with politicians old and young. True to the Acland family tradition, Sir Francis was an active Liberal statesman and Eleanor a dedicated party member. Enthusiastic supporters called Killerton 'the Castle Beautiful of Liberalism'.

Killerton is surrounded by a wonderful garden, full of rare trees and shrubs. Huge herbaceous borders are particularly spectacular in July and August but the garden is open the year round and there is always something to enjoy. Hidden in the grounds is a remarkable ice-house which could hold up to 40 tons of ice and 'the Bear's Hut', a delightful little rustic folly built in 1808 for Lydia, wife of the 'The Great Sir Thomas'. She created the garden early in the nineteenth century, helped by the famous nurseryman John Veitch.

Under the patriarchal rule of 'The Great Sir Thomas', Killerton and its estate flourished. He had 10 children and 37 grandchildren and was an MP for over 40 years. Among many other projects, he built Killerton Chapel, and attended Sunday service there regularly, greeting the congregation and noting absentees '. . . like the veteran father of a very large family'.

'Tom Thumb', the son who inherited Killerton in 1871, had his father's concern for the less fortunate. A practical man, he took cookery lessons to learn to make economical dishes, such as curried cold meat and giblet stew, at six (old) pence a time. Neither of these is on the menu at Killerton, but a recipe which follows for Dave's Turkey Plait continues the tradition as an excellent, economical way of dealing with left-over Christmas turkey.

The house and garden are still the centre of the thriving estate, and menus take account of the good fresh local vegetables and fruit available. Do go and enjoy the good food in the elegant dining-room with its large french windows which offer a further bonus of a view of the glorious garden.

Red Pepper Soup

1 oz/25 g butter
1 medium onion, finely chopped
3 red peppers
3 tomatoes
1¾ pints/1 litre vegetable stock
1 teaspoon sugar
Salt and pepper to taste
Fromage frais and fresh basil to
  garnish

Melt the butter in a large saucepan and sauté the chopped onion until it is soft. Roughly chop the peppers and the tomatoes, add to the onion and cook gently for another 5 minutes. Add the vegetable stock and sugar, bring to the boil and simmer for 30 minutes.

Liquidise the mixture until it is smooth, season with salt and pepper and serve immediately with a spoonful of fromage frais in each bowl and a little chopped basil.

This soup has a subtle, slightly smoky flavour. It is also delicious served chilled with the same garnish.

Dave's Turkey Plait

12 oz/350 g puff or shortcrust
  pastry
1 tablespoon sunflower oil
1 small onion, chopped
2 oz/50 g button mushrooms
14 oz/400 g tin chopped
  tomatoes
8 oz/225 g cooked, diced turkey
8 oz/225 g cooked diced potatoes
  (preferably a waxy or salad
  variety)
Salt and black pepper to taste
Egg and milk to glaze

Preheat oven to 220°C, 425°F, gas mark 7. Roll the pastry into a large rectangle approx. 15 in × 10 in/37 cm × 25 cm. Place it on a piece of baking paper and allow to rest while you prepare the filling.

Heat the oil and sauté the onion until soft, add the mushrooms, stir and add the chopped tomatoes. Allow to bubble for 5 minutes or so to reduce and thicken the sauce. Cool.

Lay the potatoes down the centre of the pastry, leaving sufficient pastry on each side to meet over the top and enough at the ends to seal the plait. Then put the turkey on the potatoes and finish with the sauce. Brush the uncovered pastry with the egg glaze and cut the edges into 1½ in/4 cm wide strips. Fold these strips up over the filling, criss-crossing them in the centre to give the effect of a plait. Turn up the ends to enclose the filling. Brush the whole plait with egg glaze. Bake for approx. 20 to 30 minutes until golden brown. The paper makes it easier to transfer the plait to a dish for cutting and serving.

There are echoes of that West Country speciality, the pasty, in the inclusion of potato in this tasty way of using cooked turkey.

Killerton Chocolate Pot

4 tablespoons cocoa
8 oz/225 g soft brown sugar
Boiling water to mix
1 tablespoon Grand Marnier or
    Cointreau
1 pint/500 ml double cream
Grated orange zest to garnish

Mix the cocoa and sugar into a thick paste with boiling water. Leave to cool, then chill in the fridge until really cold. Put the liqueur and cocoa mixture in a mixing bowl. Using an electric rotary whisk, beat in the cream slowly, being careful not to overbeat the mixture. When all is combined, fill small ramekins with the chocolate mixture and garnish with grated orange zest. This is very rich and creamy and keeps excellently for a day or two in the fridge.

This is often on the menu at Killerton – by special request of regular visitors.

Cherry Chip Biscuits

4 oz/125 g soft brown sugar
8 oz/225 g butter or margarine
12 oz/350 g plain flour
4 oz/125 g glacé cherries,
    chopped

Preheat oven to 180°C, 350F, gas mark 4. Either grease a baking sheet or line it with baking paper. Cream the sugar and butter together until soft, light and fluffy. Work in the flour to make a soft mixture and stir in the chopped cherries. Place a dessertspoonful of the mixture on the prepared tray. Flatten the tops with a fork. Bake for 15 to 20 minutes, until golden brown. Cool on a wire tray.

Very good served with the Killerton Chocolate Pot.

LANHYDROCK
CORNWALL

Built of grey granite, set in a secluded Cornish valley, Lanhydrock's apparently seventeenth-century exterior conceals a much more recent building. The Robartes family built Lanhydrock just before the Civil War, but a disastrous fire on 4 April 1881 destroyed most of the old house except the north wing.

Thomas Charles Robartes, 'the little lord', immediately rebuilt it and lived there quietly and happily with his large family for the next forty years. The only reminders now of the fire are the numbers of shiny brass fire hydrants and the neatly coiled hoses installed wherever possible.

The house we see today is a remarkably preserved example of what a Victorian landowner considered necessary, both 'above' and 'below' stairs, to pursue a modest and unostentatious life. 'Above stairs', apart from the magnificent Long Gallery that survived the fire, there are bedrooms, dressing-rooms and sitting-rooms of every size, a billiard room, a gunroom and a smoking room for gentlemen, a boudoir for ladies, day and night nurseries and a schoolroom for the children. There is a library that doubled as a music room, a prayer room and separate rooms from which Lord and Lady Robartes ran their respective parts of the estate and household.

'Below stairs' begins outside the big panelled dining-room with the china closet, the butler's pantry, the wine cellar and the serving room. A small army of servants was needed to run this house, and we have a rare opportunity here to see their lives in detail. Every room had its special function and is furnished accordingly.

Cooks may want to linger in the heart of this world, the Great Kitchen. This huge double-storey room was the domain of the cook, her assistant cooks and scullery maids. High up, pivoted windows ensure that food remained fresh and that smells and heat were quickly removed. On one wall is a complicated roasting spit operated by a fan in the flue, on another an immense range for boiling and simmering. There are ovens for soufflés and fine baking, and a copper bain-marie for custards and sauces. Beyond are attendant sculleries, dairy, meat, fish and dry larders, still-room and bakehouse. The dairy has slate and marble slabs cooled by a continuous stream of water from a hillside spring. In the dairy scullery next door, there is a special scalding range for producing that delicious West Country speciality, clotted cream.

On the first and second floors you will find the world of footmen, parlour maids and the personal servants, valets and ladies' maids. There are special rooms for luggage, for ironing and mending and for linen. Water jugs and tidy boxes of cleaning equipment are neatly lined up in the housemaids' closet.

If all this efficiency seems too much, revive yourself in the restaurants which occupy the old servants' hall and housekeeper's quarters. Cornish teas, of course, feature local clotted cream, lunch menus are ample and imaginative.

Spicy Parsnip Soup

4oz/125g butter
1 large onion, chopped
2 cloves garlic
1 teaspoon turmeric
1 teaspoon coriander seeds
1 teaspoon cumin
¼ teaspoon fenugreek
1lb/450g parsnips, peeled and
    chopped
1 medium potato, peeled and
    chopped
1½ pints/750ml water
1 fresh chilli
1 teaspoon sugar
Salt to taste

GARNISH
Single cream
Chopped parsley
Garlic croûtons

Melt the butter in a large pan, sauté the onion and garlic for 5 to 10 minutes, then add the turmeric, coriander seeds, cumin and fenugreek. Cook gently for 5 minutes. Add the parsnips and potato. Stir well to blend in and sauté for a further 5 minutes. Add the water, bring to the boil and simmer until the parsnips and potato are cooked. Blend the soup until smooth. Return to the pan, add the chilli, simmer gently for 10 minutes. Remove the chilli. Add the sugar and salt to taste. Serve garnished with a swirl of cream, chopped parsley and garlic croûtons.

The sweetness of the parsnips complements the spices perfectly. A delicious example of Indian spices enhancing English ingredients.

Cheese and Onion Pie

12oz/350g shortcrust pastry
    made with half wholemeal
    and half plain flour

FILLING
8oz/225g Cheddar cheese cut
    into ¼in/5mm slices
3oz/75g butter
3 large onions, peeled and sliced
½ pint/250ml milk
Pepper and salt to taste
Egg wash
Sesame seeds
A little extra grated cheese

Preheat oven to 160°C, 325°F, gas mark 3. Roll out two-thirds of the pastry and use to line a 9in/23cm springform tin. Cover the pastry with half the cheese slices. Melt butter and sauté the onions until soft. Add the milk, season to taste and allow to cool. Spread this mixture over the cheese slices. Cover with the remaining cheese slices. Roll out the remaining pastry and use to cover the pie. Brush the edges with egg wash and seal them, then make a hole in the centre. Brush the top with egg wash, and scatter with sesame seeds and grated cheese. Bake for approx. 1 hour, to allow the pastry base to cook as well as the top. If the top looks as if it is browning too fast, cover with foil for the rest of the cooking time.

Baked Aubergine and Tomato Layer

2 large aubergines
Salt
Approx. ¼ pint/150ml
    sunflower oil
2 tablespoons olive oil
1oz/25g butter
1 clove garlic, crushed
1 onion, peeled and chopped
1 tablespoon tomato purée
14oz/400g tin tomatoes
½ teaspoon oregano
1 teaspoon sugar
1 tablespoon chopped fresh
    basil
Salt and pepper to taste
2oz/50g grated Gruyère cheese

Preheat oven to 180°C, 350°F, gas mark 4. Slice aubergines, salt well and leave to stand for at least 30 minutes. Meanwhile make the tomato sauce as follows. Heat the butter and olive oil and fry the garlic and onion for 5 minutes. (It should still be crunchy.) Add the tomato purée, tinned tomatoes, oregano and sugar. Simmer for a further 5 minutes, add the fresh basil, check seasoning, add pepper and salt to taste.

Drain and rinse the aubergines. Dry on kitchen paper and then fry in the sunflower oil until golden brown on both sides. Drain on more kitchen paper.

In a gratin dish layer the aubergine slices and tomato sauce. Top with grated Gruyère cheese and put in the oven for just as much time as it takes for the cheese to melt, brown and bubble.

Serve with baked or new potatoes and a salad.

Broccoli and Cauliflower in Stilton Sauce

12oz/350g broccoli florets
12oz/350g cauliflower florets
3oz/75g butter
3oz/75g plain flour
1 dessertspoon Dijon mustard
½ pint/250ml water
1 pint/500ml milk
3oz/75g Cheddar cheese, grated
6oz/175g Stilton, crumbled or
    grated

Boil or steam the broccoli and cauliflower florets until tender, taking care that they do not overcook. Drain, retain the cooking liquid and make it up to ½ pint/250ml if necessary. Mix the vegetables together in a serving dish. Cover and put in a warm oven to keep hot while you make the sauce.

Melt the butter, stir in the flour and cook for 5 minutes, stirring constantly. Add first the mustard and then the milk and vegetable water alternately, stirring as you do so to avoid lumps. Bring to the boil and simmer for 10 minutes, stirring hard. (This is the secret of a good sauce, constant stirring and a sufficient time to cook the flour in the sauce.) Take the pan off the heat, add the grated cheese, stir until it is blended and season to taste with pepper. It should not need salt as Stilton is a salty cheese. Pour over the hot vegetables and serve immediately.

Steamed Chocolate Sponge

4oz/125g butter
4oz/125g caster sugar
3 eggs
4oz/125g sifted self-raising flour
2oz/50g sifted cocoa
2 tablespoons golden syrup

Butter a 1 pint/500ml pudding basin. Cream together butter and sugar until pale and fluffy. Beat in eggs, adding a spoonful of flour with each egg. Fold in the remaining flour and the cocoa. Spoon the syrup into the bottom of the basin and top with the mixture. Smooth the surface and cover with greaseproof paper and foil. Steam for 80 minutes.

Towards the end of the cooking time, prepare the Rich Chocolate Sauce (below). When the pudding is done, turn it on to a plate and serve the sauce separately.

Rich Chocolate Sauce

4oz/125g plain chocolate
1oz/25g butter
1oz/25g sugar
Milk
1 tablespoon Madeira
    (Cointreau or Grand Marnier
    are acceptable substitutes)

Put all the ingredients except the Madeira in a bowl and set the bowl over a saucepan of gently simmering water. Allow them to melt together, stirring all the time. When melted, add the Madeira. If you do not wish to serve it immediately, it can be cooled and reheated by the same method. (Don't worry if it solidifies on cooling.)

MONTACUTE
SOMERSET

Montacute is a great, golden Elizabethan house, built in the 1590s by Sir Edward Phelips with the help of a Somerset mason, William Arnold. The façade is both impressive and theatrically beautiful. Arnold incorporated all the fashionable details of the Renaissance: classical statues in shell-headed niches, obelisks and a symmetrical plan.

Sir Edward would have received his guests in the Great Hall from which a monumental stone staircase leads to the Great Chamber on the first floor. The same route would have been taken by the formal procession of food from the kitchen to the Great Chamber, where Sir Edward dined in state. Arnold also incorporated another current fashion: an exquisite little Banqueting House in a corner of the East Court. Here the company would retire after dinner for the final dessert course of 'banquet' delicacies – marchpane, crystallised quince paste and gingerbread were favourites.

As the Phelips family's fortunes waxed and waned over the next three centuries, so did those of their house. Sometimes Montacute was richly furnished, sometimes neglected. What is certain, however, is that life in the big house can never have been as bleak as that of the labourers on the estate's farms in the difficult years of the early nineteenth century. This is an extract from an autobiographical account by George Mitchell, who lived locally, written during the 1830s.

Our food consisted principally of a little barley-cake, potatoes, salt and barley 'flippet'. Tea kettle broth consisted of a few pieces of bread soaked in hot water with a little salt, sometimes with a leek chopped up in it. Never had I ever a sufficient quantity of bread being used for the spoon to stand upright in. Barley flippet was made by sprinkling barley-meal into a pot of boiling water which when sufficiently thickened, was served up with salt and a little treacle.

Sometimes, I would pull a turnip from the field and gnaw it to prevent hunger . . . and many a time have I hunted and foraged about for snails in the hedges and roasted them for my lunch and tea.

Today, visitors to Montacute are luckier. Carefully cooked, affordable dishes are available for all in the old laundry and bakehouse, now the restaurant.

Smoky Sausage Casserole

1 tablespoon vegetable oil
1 lb/450 g traditional pork and smoked bacon sausages
1 large onion, peeled and sliced
1 large carrot, peeled and sliced
1 lb/450 g potatoes, peeled and diced
2 tablespoons tomato purée
7½ oz/215 g tin black-eyed beans, drained and rinsed
7½ oz/215 g tin red kidney beans, drained and rinsed
2 tablespoons wholegrain mustard
1 pint/500 ml beef bouillon
2 oz/50 g Savoy cabbage, finely shredded

Heat the oil in a large saucepan or a heavy-based casserole and fry the sausages gently for 10 to 15 minutes. Add the onion, carrot and potato and fry for a further 5 minutes, until the onion is soft. Stir in the tomato purée, the beans, mustard and beef stock. Bring to the boil, reduce the heat and simmer gently for 20 minutes, stirring occasionally. Stir in the cabbage and cook for a further 5 minutes.

Country Turkey Pie

PASTRY
12 oz/350g plain flour
1 teaspoon salt
1 teaspoon mixed herbs
4 oz/125g butter
2 oz/50g white vegetable fat
1 egg

FILLING
1 lb/450g minced turkey meat
*6 oz/175g smoked bacon,
    rindless and finely chopped*
*1 medium onion, peeled and
    chopped*
*2 oz/50g fresh white
    breadcrumbs*
*3 tablespoons medium dry
    sherry*
1 tablespoon chopped parsley
*1 small cooking apple, peeled,
    cored and chopped*
1 egg, beaten

Preheat oven to 200°C, 400°F, gas mark 6. Sift the flour and salt into a bowl. Stir in herbs, then rub in the fats until the mixture resembles fine breadcrumbs. Add egg and 5–6 tablespoons water and mix to a soft (but not sticky) dough. Knead lightly, then wrap and chill in the fridge for 30 minutes.

Mix turkey, bacon, onion, breadcrumbs, sherry, parsley and apple in a big bowl. Reserve a little of the beaten egg to brush the pastry and mix the rest into the filling.

Lightly grease an 8 in/20 cm springform tin. Roll out ⅔ of the pastry to a circle approx. 15 in/37 cm wide. Fold in half and use to line the tin. Press well down, then spoon the turkey mixture into the tin, levelling the top. Roll out the remaining pastry, dampen the inside edge and fit on top of the pie. Trim the edges and seal. Pierce a hole in the centre of the top and use any extra pastry trimmings to decorate it. Brush the top with beaten egg. Bake for 20 minutes in the preheated oven, then reduce the temperature to 180°C, 350°F, gas mark 4 and cook for a further 40 minutes. If the pastry top gets too brown, cover with greaseproof paper.

Serve hot or cold. Very good for a picnic.

Spinach Pie

8 in/20 cm shortcrust pastry case

FILLING
*1 lb/450g spinach, washed and
    chopped*
2 oz/50g butter
8 oz/225g cottage cheese
3 eggs
*4 oz/125g mature Cheddar
    cheese*
*Salt, pepper and grated nutmeg
    to taste*

Preheat oven to 190°C, 375°F, gas mark 5. Melt the butter and sauté the spinach in it for a few minutes until it begins to wilt. Then set aside to cool. Mix together the cottage and Cheddar cheeses, eggs and seasoning. Stir in the spinach and pile into the pastry case. Bake for approx. 30 minutes, or until set.

Serve either at room temperature or warm. The flavours seem to intensify if the pie cools a little.

Baked Almond Pudding

1 oz/25 g butter
10 fl oz/300 ml single cream
10 fl oz/300 ml milk
Grated rind of lemon
1 piece of cinnamon stick
1 blade mace or pinch of
  powdered mace
3 oz/75 g caster sugar
6 oz/175 g fresh white
  breadcrumbs
4 oz/125 g ground almonds
4 oz/125 g almond biscuits,
  broken into small pieces
  (use Amaretti or something
  similar with a good flavour)
4 eggs
½ teaspoon grated nutmeg
Pinch of salt

Preheat oven to 190°C, 375°F, gas mark 5. Butter a 9in/23cm gratin dish. Bring the cream and milk to the boil, reduce the heat and add the lemon rind, cinnamon stick, mace and sugar. Stir well and simmer for 10 minutes. Mix the breadcrumbs, ground almonds and almond biscuits in a large bowl and pour in the milk and cream mixture through a sieve. Mix thoroughly and allow to cool to lukewarm. Beat the eggs until foamy, add nutmeg and salt and stir into the almond mixture. Pour into the gratin dish and bake for approx. 45 minutes until firm. This pudding has an equally good variation (below).

STEAMED ALMOND PUDDING

Butter a 2 pint/1200ml pudding basin. Add 1 tablespoon candied peel and 1 tablespoon currants to the mixture given above. Pour into the basin. Cover with a layer of grease-proof paper and one of foil, tucking the latter in under the rim of the bowl. Place in a saucepan filled with water to come half way up the basin and simmer for 1¾ hours. Turn out and serve at once.

At Montacute, Steamed Almond Pudding is served with ice-cream or cream but Baked Almond Pudding is delicious served warm from the oven on its own.

Toffee Apple Crumble

PASTRY
8 oz/225 g plain flour
4 tablespoons caster sugar
4 oz/125 g butter
4 egg yolks

FILLING
2 lb/900 g cooking apples, peeled
* and thinly sliced*

TOFFEE SAUCE
2 oz/50 g butter
2 oz/50 g granulated sugar
3 oz/75 g soft brown sugar
5 fl oz/125 ml golden syrup
5 fl oz/125 ml double cream
2 drops vanilla essence

CRUMBLE
4 oz/125 g flour
4 oz/125 g porridge oats
3 oz/75 g butter
3 oz/75 g soft brown sugar

Preheat oven to 180°C, 350°F, gas mark 4. First line a greased 10 in/25 cm flan tin with pastry made as follows. Sift flour with the sugar, rub in butter and stir in the egg yolks to bind the dough. Roll out, line flan tin and prick the bottom. Chill while you prepare the filling and the crumble.

Peel and slice the apples thinly. Arrange on the bottom of the pastry case. Melt the butter and dissolve the sugars and the syrup over a very low heat. Cook very gently, stirring well for 5 minutes. Remove the pan from the heat and stir in the cream and the vanilla. Beat well until the sauce is smooth. Let it cool to lukewarm, then pour it over the apples. To make the crumble, rub the butter into the flour and oats until the mixture is crumbly, stir in the sugar and spread the mixture evenly over the filling. Bake for approx. 30 to 40 minutes. The top should be golden and crunchy.

This is also delicious made with pears.

MOUNT STEWART
CO. DOWN

Twelve miles south of Belfast, at the head of Strangford Lough, sheltered from the cold north wind, nurtured by heavy night dews and close to the Gulf Stream, lies the mansion of Mount Stewart.

This is the home of the Londonderry family, Anglo-Irish aristocrats and politicians for three centuries. The house we see today is mainly the work of William Morrison, commissioned in the 1830s by the 3rd Marquess. It is imposing, topped with a heavy balustrade and built of dark grey local stone. However, it is neither oppressive nor overwhelming. This is because the extraordinary gardens, formal yet lush, full of colour and surprising statuary, provide a perfect setting contrasting with the elegant formality of the buildings. The whole exotic effect of the garden is quite magical, which is entirely appropriate since it is the creation of Circe the Sorceress, otherwise Edith, wife of the 7th Marquess.

Edith was beautiful, energetic and a brilliant hostess. During the First World War, not content with establishing the Women's Legion, for which she was made a Dame, she also founded the Ark Club for her friends. Circe (Edith) presided over informal dinners where those engaged in war work could relax. Every member was given the name of a bird, a beast or a mythical character. Her husband was Charley the Cheetah, Winston Churchill a warlock, Nancy Astor (see Cliveden) a gnat.

When she came to the house as a bride at the turn of the century, Edith wrote that she found it 'the dampest darkest and saddest place I had ever stayed in'. After her husband inherited Mount Stewart in 1915 she transformed it. Inside the house her influence is most evident in the bedrooms, which are all named after European cities. 'Rome' is painted a dramatic deep gold, the lights are huge brass candlesticks and the bed is carved and painted. The gardens, which she laid out in the 1920s, reflect her eclectic tastes. Strolling along the Fountain Walk beneath eucalyptus trees a hundred feet high or sitting under the clipped arches of cypress in the Spanish Garden, it is difficult to believe that one is still in the British Isles. Amongst the rosemary, lavender and camellias of the Dodo Terrace you can find the Ark Club immortalised in stone. Her husband, Charley the Cheetah, is there of course, but which humans inspired the dodos and the dinosaurs?

Circe, surrounded by more animal Ark members, is present in Naomi McBride's delightful mural in the tea-room where you can enjoy Ulster scones or home-made cakes. The salad recipes are used in buffets served in the Temple of the Winds, the exquisite banqueting house which the 3rd Marquess described as 'a Temple built for mirth and Jollity . . . solely appropriate for a Junketing Retreat in the grounds'. Sentiments echoed, I am sure, by anyone lucky enough to have partied there.

Rough Puff Chicken Pie

8 oz/225 g plain flour
6 oz/175 g butter
Salt, pepper and chilli powder
Water to mix
2 oz/50 g butter
4 oz/125 g button mushrooms
2 oz/50 g plain flour
½ pint/250 ml creamy milk
½ pint/250 ml chicken stock
8 oz/225 g diced cooked chicken
4 oz/125 g sweetcorn, frozen or
   tinned
1 tablespoon finely chopped
   parsley
A little extra milk

About two hours before you start, put the first 6 oz/150 g of butter in the freezer.

Preheat oven to 220°C, 425°F, gas mark 7. Sift the flour with salt, pepper and a pinch of chilli powder. Grate the frozen butter and mix half with the flour. Use cold water to make a firm dough. Roll out the dough to a rectangle approx. 14 in × 6 in/35 cm × 15 cm. Scatter the second half of grated butter over the sheet and fold as if making an envelope. Turn the sheet once and roll it to the same size as before. Allow the pastry to rest for 5 to 10 minutes. Then turn it again, fold it as before and roll it. Repeat this twice more, so that you will have rolled and folded four times.

Melt a third of the remaining 2 oz/50 g of butter and gently sauté the mushrooms in it. Use the remaining butter, flour, milk and stock to make a béchamel sauce. Stir into this sauce the mushrooms and juices, the diced chicken, sweetcorn and parsley.

Season to taste and put on to an ovenproof plate. Roll out the pastry and cut to fit the top, using the scraps left over to make pastry leaves as decoration. Brush with milk and bake approx. 20 to 30 minutes, until the pastry is golden brown.

Broccoli, Pepper and Pear Salad

2 heads broccoli
1 red pepper
1 yellow pepper
1 green pepper
2 firm ripe pears

DRESSING
4 tablespoons olive oil
1 tablespoon wine vinegar
Salt and pepper to taste

Divide the broccoli into florets and blanch for a couple of minutes in boiling water, drain and refresh with cold water to stop the colour becoming dull. Put them in a salad bowl. De-seed and chop the peppers and add to the broccoli. Combine the oil and vinegar, salt and pepper to make the dressing. Peel and slice the pears, toss in the dressing, add dressing and pears to the broccoli and peppers and mix well.

The brilliant colours of this salad are matched by the crunchy contrasts in flavours and texture.

Waldorf Salad

4 large sticks of celery
4 green apples
6oz/175g green grapes
2oz/50g walnut pieces
Sesame seeds or toasted pine
　　nuts to garnish

DRESSING
3 tablespoons Greek-style
　　yoghurt
Squeeze of lemon juice
3 tablespoons mayonnaise
Salt and pepper to taste

Clean and chop the celery. Try to use Granny Smith apples for this recipe, as they do not discolour quickly. Core and chop them. Pip the grapes and cut in half if they are large. Mix all these and the walnuts together in a salad bowl.

Combine the yoghurt, with the lemon juice and mayonnaise and season. Pour over the salad and mix well. Sprinkle with sesame seeds or toasted pine nuts.

Walnut Carrot Cake with Cream Cheese Topping

8oz/225g self-raising flour
2 level teaspoons baking
　　powder
6oz/175g light soft brown sugar
2oz/50g chopped walnuts
4oz/125g carrots, peeled and
　　grated
2 ripe bananas, mashed
Small tin of crushed pineapple
　　(approx. 7½oz/215g)
2 eggs, well beaten
¼ pint/150ml sunflower oil

CREAM CHEESE TOPPING
3oz/75g softened butter
3oz/75g full-fat cream cheese
6oz/175g sieved icing sugar
½ teaspoon vanilla essence

Preheat oven to 180°C, 350°F, gas mark 4. Either grease and flour or line with greaseproof paper an 8in/20cm loose-bottomed cake tin. Sift the flour and baking powder into a mixing bowl large enough to take all ingredients and to allow you to beat the mixture. Stir in the sugar, nuts, grated carrot, mashed banana and pineapple. Make a well in the centre of the mixture, add the eggs and oil and beat well for 5 minutes. Pour into the prepared tin and bake for approx. 1¼ hours, until golden brown. Take out of the tin and cool on a wire tray.

Place butter, cream cheese, icing sugar and vanilla essence in a bowl. Beat until smooth. Spread over cooled cake and rough up with a fork. Chill for an hour or so to allow the icing to harden before serving.

Ulster Scones

9oz/250g *wholemeal flour*
9oz/250g *strong white flour*
½ teaspoon *bicarbonate of soda*
3oz/75g *sugar*
3oz/75g *margarine*
1 egg, *beaten*
12fl oz/360ml *buttermilk*

OPTIONAL
2oz/50g *chopped glacé cherries*
   or 2oz/50g *sultanas*

Preheat oven to 220°C, 425°F, gas mark 7. Grease or line a baking sheet with baking paper. Sift the two flours together with the bicarbonate of soda and sugar. (If you are making fruit scones, add the cherries or sultanas at this point and mix them in well.) Rub in the margarine. Stir in the buttermilk and egg and knead the mixture until it forms a soft dough. *Do not overwork the dough.* Roll the dough out to about 1in/3cm thick and cut the scones into rounds or triangles. This should make about 2 dozen. Brush the tops with milk and bake 10 to 15 minutes, until golden brown and risen.

In Ulster you can buy soda bread flour, which is a combination of brown and white. I asked my daughter, married to an Irishman, for the proportion she uses, which I have given here, but really, it is a matter of personal taste and what works for you. It is a hotbed of controversy in Ireland, where cooks are assessed on their breads and everyone has a different key to success.

Ulster Cheese Cakes

8oz/225g *shortcrust pastry*
Strawberry or raspberry jam
6oz/175g *butter or margarine*
6oz/175g *caster sugar*
6oz/175g *plain flour*
3 eggs, *well beaten*

Preheat oven to 160°C, 325°F, gas mark 3. Roll out the pastry and use to line small tartlet tins brushed with sunflower oil. Prick the bottoms and leave to rest while making the filling. Cream the butter and sugar together until light and fluffy. Beat in the eggs gradually, adding a little flour if the mixture should start to curdle. Then fold in the remaining flour.

Place a small teaspoon of jam on each pastry base and fill with sponge mix. Bake for approximately 20 minutes, until golden brown. Allow to cool and dust with caster sugar before serving.

OXBURGH HALL
NORFOLK

The Bedingfeld family have always been both Royalists and Catholic. Oxburgh Hall has been their home for five hundred years and members of the family still live in part of this beautiful house. Their history is as much part of its fabric as the bricks and mortar of its mellow red walls.

It appears to be a castle with crenellated towers, a gatehouse and a moat, but although fifteenth-century Norfolk was turbulent, Oxburgh was not built to withstand siege and bombardment. It was a fortified manor appropriate for a gentleman of substance.

Through the centuries, the Bedingfelds served successive monarchs loyally in different roles. Some of these were extremely delicate. Sir Edmund Bedingfeld was steward to Catherine of Aragon after Henry VIII divorced her: his son Henry served Queen Mary Tudor by acting as jailer to her half-sister, the Princess Elizabeth. Luckily Elizabeth seemed to bear him no ill will, and visitors can still see an apparently amicable letter written to him by the Queen after her accession.

During the next three hundred years, the fortunes of the Bedingfelds fluctuated according to the current attitudes to their faith. As staunch Catholics, they endured persecution, heavy fines and restrictions. We can still see the entrance to a claustrophobic priest's hole, a reminder of those difficult years. However, most of the rooms visited now are the result of happier times. They are exuberantly Victorian, reflecting the relief that the Catholic Emancipation Act of 1829 brought. The walls glow with brightly coloured wallpapers and embossed leather; huge pieces of furniture incorporate medieval and contemporary carving. Now allowed a place of worship, the 6th Baronet, Sir Henry Paston-Bedingfeld, built in the grounds a chapel which is also full of colour and carving.

Appropriately for a house so full of history, historic recipes and traditional ingredients feature on the menu. The kitchen garden is now planted with old varieties of fruit trees: quinces, plums and medlars. There are two recipes for quinces, with their flavour as distinctive as Oxburgh's vivid Victorian wall-coverings. A delicious Cheese Pudding is enhanced by a handful of fresh herbs from the kitchen garden and the Beef and Vegetable Pottage, a modern version of a medieval staple, uses the root vegetables which grow so well in the rich Norfolk soil.

Beef and Vegetable Pottage

2 lb/900 g prepared vegetables
1½ lb/675 g shin of beef
Vegetable stock
2 tablespoons fresh mixed herbs
    or 1 tablespoon mixed dried
    herbs

Preheat oven to 160°C, 325°F, gas mark 3. Prepare a mix of roughly chopped vegetables of some of the following: leeks, celery, onions, carrots, turnips, cabbage. Chop the meat into large chunks and pack it at the bottom of a large cast-iron casserole. Add the herbs and sufficient vegetable stock to cover the meat and bring to the boil on the top of the stove. Take the casserole off the heat and add all the chopped vegetables in a thick layer on top of the meat and stock. Cover the pan and cook slowly in the oven for at least 2 and preferably 3 hours. Simmer the pot on the top of the stove for the last half an hour if you are serving with Norfolk Dumpling (below), so it can bake in a hotter oven. Season with salt if necessary and serve each helping topped with a wedge of dumpling.

This is a rich man's pottage since it contains meat. See the recipe for Pease Pottage on p.53 for a poor man's version. Pottage was eaten by everyone in the Middle Ages. Notice there are no potatoes in the recipe – they hadn't yet reached Britain.

Baked Norfolk Dumpling

8 oz/225 g self-raising flour
Pinch of salt
6 oz/175 g shredded suet
Milk

Grease a 9 in/23 cm flan dish. Mix together the flour, salt and shredded suet with just enough milk to make a soft dough. Knead the dough into a round, approx. 1 in/2.5 cm thick, and place in the dish. Make criss-cross lines on the top and brush with milk. Turn the oven up to 190°C, 375°F, gas mark 5 and bake the dumpling for 30 to 40 minutes. Cut into wedges to serve with the pottage.

Norfolk Dumplings were traditionally eaten with gravy before the meal as a filler – in the same way as Yorkshire Pudding. They were also boiled and served as a dessert with jam, treacle or butter and sugar. This recipe comes from a book of traditional Norfolk recipes compiled by Molly Perham.

Pickled Herring and Fruit Pie

PASTRY
12 oz/350g plain flour
Salt and black pepper
3 oz/75g butter
3 oz/75g lard
Cold water to mix

FILLING
1 lb/450g pickled herrings or
* roll mops*
1 large cooking pear, peeled,
* cored and sliced*
1 oz/25g raisins
1 oz/25g currants
2 oz/50g dates, pitted and
* minced*
Pinch of salt
¼ teaspoon ground cinnamon
2 tablespoons dry white wine
1 oz/25g butter, cut into small
* pieces*
Beaten egg, or milk, to glaze
1 teaspoon sugar

Preheat oven to 220°C, 425°F, gas mark 7. To make the pastry, sieve the flour and salt together into a bowl. Add a sprinkling of pepper, then rub in the butter and lard until the mixture resembles fine breadcrumbs. Mix with enough cold water to make a firm dough. Knead lightly until smooth. Divide into two portions, about two-thirds and one-third. Roll out the two portions and then chill them for about 10 minutes.

Grease a deep 8 in/20 cm flan tin and line it with the larger portion of pastry. Bake blind for 10 minutes. Leave to cool. Reduce the temperature of the oven to 190°C, 375°F, gas mark 5.

Meanwhile, prepare the filling. Unroll the herrings if necessary. Remove any onions and reserve. Rinse the herrings in cold water and drain. Plunge them into 3 pints/1.7 litres boiling water in a saucepan, cook for 1 minute, remove and drain well. Cut into chunks.

Mix the pear, dried fruit, salt, cinnamon and wine together in a bowl and add the herring and the reserved onions. Transfer the filling into the pastry-lined flan tin, using a slotted spoon to drain off any excess liquid. Dot the mixture with the butter and cover with the remaining pastry. Decorate the top with any pastry trimmings, then brush with the egg or milk. Make a slit in the top to allow the steam to escape and sprinkle with the sugar. Bake for 1 hour, or until golden brown.

Although this Norfolk recipe, which first appeared in *The Art of Dining*, may seem odd to modern eyes, it is greeted (and eaten!) enthusiastically whenever it is served at Elizabethan banquets at Oxburgh.

Cheese Pudding

½ pint/250ml milk
10oz/300g soft white
  breadcrumbs
6oz/175g mature Cheddar
  cheese, grated
7oz/200g melted butter
4 eggs
Pinch of salt and pepper
2 tablespoons fresh mixed herbs
  or 1 tablespoon mixed dried
  herbs

Preheat oven to 190°C, 375°F, gas mark 5. Butter an 8in/20cm china soufflé or gratin dish. Pour the milk on to the breadcrumbs in a bowl large enough to take all the ingredients. Stir in the melted butter and grated cheese. Beat the eggs until they are nicely frothy, about 5 minutes, and fold them into the mixture together with the herbs. Season to taste. Pour into the buttered dish and bake for about 20 minutes. Serve hot accompanied by a green salad and, if possible, a home-made pickle as a relish. At Oxburgh, this is usually a plum chutney but the apple and onion chutney (p.144) would also be excellent.

This tasty dish is Oxburgh Hall's adaptation of Michael Barry's modern version of a recipe dated 1818, originally noted at Goudhurst in Kent. An example of how inspiration travels down the centuries and across counties!

A Salad of Herbs and Flowers

'Take your herbs and pick them very fine into fine water, and pick your flowers by themselves and wash them clean, then swing them in a strainer, and when you put them into a dish, mingle them with cucumbers or lemons pared and sliced, also scrape sugar, and put in vinegar and oil, then throw the flowers on the top of the salad, and of every sort of the aforesaid things and garnish the dish about, then take eggs boiled hard, and lay about the dish and upon the salad.'

This recipe for an Elizabethan salad comes from *The Good Huswife's Jewell* by Thomas Dawson, published in 1596. At Oxburgh this salad was made as part of an Elizabethan banquet held in the spring. It consisted of Welsh onions, shallots, sage, rosemary, thyme, parsley, chives and bay garnished with cowslips, primroses and violets, all from the garden. Only the eggs were not home produced!

Baked Quinces in Honey

10oz/300g honey
½ pint/250ml orange or
    grapefruit juice
6 quinces, peeled, cored and
    quartered

Preheat oven to 160°C, 325°F, gas mark 3. Mix the honey into the fruit juice. Lay the quince quarters into a casserole or gratin dish and pour over the liquid. It should well cover them. Put in the oven and bake until the quinces are tender which will take about 2 hours. Check the dish after an hour or so and if they are getting too dry, add a little water and cover the dish with a lid or foil for the rest of cooking time. Allow to cool and serve cold. The grainy texture of the quinces provides a good contrast to the sweet syrup.

Quince Salami

2-2½lb/1 generous kilo large
    quinces, thinly peeled
1¾lb/850g caster sugar
Juice of 1 lemon
6oz/175g mixed crystallised
    fruits, such as cherries,
    pineapple, pears, apricots and
    plums, chopped if large
8oz/225g blanched almonds,
    roughly chopped

Put the quinces in a large saucepan, cover with water and bring to the boil. Boil, covered, until the quinces are soft (this may take quite a long time). Remove the saucepan from the heat and place the fruit in a colander to drain. Reserve the cooking liquid. While they are still hot, core the quinces and purée them in a food processor or blender.

Measure 8 fl oz/225 ml of the cooking liquid into a saucepan. Reserve two tablespoons of sugar and dissolve the rest in the liquid over a very low heat. Stir continuously until the syrup is clear, then bring it to the boil without stirring and let it boil for a minute or two until it thickens. Add the quince purée and continue cooking and stirring until the mixture becomes very thick and leaves the side of the pan. Remove the saucepan from the heat, stir in the lemon juice, the crystallised fruits and almonds. Stir until they are well distributed throughout the quince paste.

Turn the mixture out on to a smooth surface and work it into a sausage shape as soon as it is cool enough to handle. Then roll it in the remaining sugar and chill it well. Slice the salami thinly and serve with after-dinner coffee instead of petits fours or truffles.

Centenary Celebration Cake

10 oz/300g plain flour
1 level teaspoon baking powder
3 level teaspoons mixed spice
6 oz/175 g caster sugar
2 oz/50 g ground almonds
6 fl oz/175 ml sunflower oil
6 fl oz/175 ml milk
3 eggs
2 oz/50 g sultanas
3 oz/75 g mixed peel
4 oz/125 g glacé cherries,
  chopped finely

ICING
4 oz/125 g icing sugar
3 teaspoons water
A drop of yellow colouring

Preheat oven to 180°C, 350°F, gas mark 4. Either grease and flour or line with baking paper a 9in/20cm cake tin.

Sieve flour, baking powder and spice into a large mixing bowl. Stir in the sugar and ground almonds. Beat together the oil, milk and eggs. Then pour the mixture into a well in the centre of the dry ingredients and blend together, mixing well. Fold in the fruit and pour into the prepared tin. Bake for approx. one hour, or until a skewer pushed into the centre of the cake comes out clean.

Remove the cake from the tin and allow to cool. When it is cold, ice as follows. Blend the sugar, water and colouring to a paste. Spread over the cake so that it covers the top and just begins to drizzle over the edge.

This cake was developed at Oxburgh to be served in all East Anglian properties during the National Trust's Centenary in 1995. Yellow was the Centenary colour – hence the yellow icing.

POWIS CASTLE
POWYS

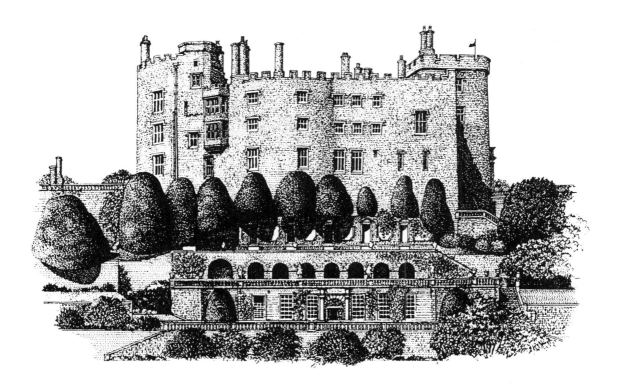

Powis is the perfect castle in the perfect setting. Although it is massive, the warm red stone means the thirteenth-century keep is impressive without being forbidding. Facing south-east, and below the great walls, are 450 feet of hanging terraces dominated by huge clipped yews, the largest surviving example of a Baroque garden in Britain. To the north is the park. Here, oak, beech, sycamore and lime are planted on 'finely unequal slopes' and 'contribute to render Powys an enviable place to the lovers of forest scenery'. So wrote the Reverend Evans on his tour of North Wales in 1802. It is just as true today.

Tear yourself away from the natural beauties of the garden and park and there are further treats in store. Visitors enter the castle from the courtyard, dominated now by Andries Carpentière's lead statue, *Fame and Pegasus*, magnificently restored. Inside are richly furnished state rooms cleverly fitted within the original medieval curtain walls. Portraits and busts of the Herbert family line the walls. The charmingly unsymmetrical Long Galley is the only Tudor survival. It was constructed and decorated by Sir Edward Herbert in 1593. His contemporary and kinsman, another Edward Herbert, is impossible to miss: there are four oil portraits, a bronze portrait bust by Le Sueur and a miniature, oil on vellum, by Isaac Oliver on view in the castle. Oliver's tiny, exquisitely detailed painting shows a beautiful young man dressed in silks and lace in the height of fashion as a 'vairy parfitt knight'. Black curly hair and a well-trimmed black beard frame his handsome face. He is reclining nonchalantly on a grassy bank in a wooded landscape rather like Powis park. In the background, a groom holds his splendid plumed helmet, beside him his white stallion, saddled and decorated, waits to whisk him off to perform deeds of courage for his fair lady. He was a poet, ambassador to Paris and was famous for writing the first secular autobiography in the English language.

A later family connection brought other treasures to Powis. 'Clive of India's' collection of ivories, textiles, gold and silver can be seen in the Clive Museum on the north side of the courtyard. In his honour, a warming Mulligatawny Soup is on the menu in the seventeenth-century stables which now form the restaurant. Alternatively, at tea time, traditional Welsh specialities such as Bara Brith (p.48) and Welsh Cakes feature.

Mulligatawny Soup

2oz/50g butter
1 large onion, peeled and
    chopped
2 carrots, peeled and chopped
1 cooking apple, peeled and
    chopped
1 tablespoon sultanas
1 tablespoon sweetish pickle
Pinch cayenne
1 teaspoon curry paste (mild or
    hot according to taste)
1 teaspoon sugar
1½ pints/750ml vegetable stock
1 dessertspoon cornflour
    (optional)
Salt and pepper to taste

Melt the butter in a largish saucepan and sauté the onion and carrots. Add the apple, sultanas and pickle. Cook gently with the lid on until the carrots are tender. Put the mixture in a food processor and process briefly – the mixture should be chunky, not a smooth purée. Return to the saucepan. Stir in the cayenne, curry paste, sugar and stock and reheat stirring all the time. If you want a thicker soup, mix the cornflour with cold water to make a thin paste and add it, and the seasoning, to the soup. Serve very hot.

Mulligatawny soup was extremely fashionable in Victoria's reign. The recipe originated in southern India, the name being an anglicised version of a Tamil word 'milagutannir' meaning pepper-water.

Sausage and Bean Hot Pot

2 tablespoons olive or
   sunflower oil
1 large onion, peeled and
   chopped
2 peppers, preferably red and
   green, de-seeded and diced
1 green chilli, de-seeded and
   finely chopped
2oz/50g button mushrooms
1 14oz/400g tin baked beans
1 7½oz/213g tin butter-beans
1 14oz/400g tin red beans
3 frankfurters, chopped into
   chunks
2 chorizos (or similar spicy
   sausages), chopped into
   chunks
1 14oz/400g tin chopped
   tomatoes
½ pint/250ml vegetable stock
2 bay leaves
Salt and pepper to taste

In a deep saucepan or cast-iron casserole, heat the oil and sauté the onion, peppers and chilli until the onion is soft. Stir in the mushrooms. Drain the tins of beans and add them with the chopped sausages, tomatoes, stock and bay leaves. Stir well to combine all the flavours, taste and season. Then put the lid on and simmer for 15 to 20 minutes before serving with crusty bread to mop up the sauce.

Powis Castle's version of a robust European favourite.

Pasta Salad Dressing

1 tablespoon cider vinegar
1 teaspoon demerara sugar
1 dessertspoon tomato purée
1 clove garlic, crushed
¼ pint/150ml olive oil
Dash of chilli
Salt to taste

Put vinegar, sugar, tomato purée and garlic in a blender. With the motor on, slowly pour in the olive oil. Season with chilli and salt. This is an excellent coating dressing for pasta or potatoes.

To vary, add basil for pasta and tomato salad; creamed horseradish for a prawn and pasta salad; mustard for a potato salad.

Normandy Gâteau

SPONGE
4 eggs
4oz/125g caster sugar
4oz/125g plain flour

FILLING
1lb/450g apples
2oz/50g sultanas
¼ pint/150ml water
2 tablespoons soft brown sugar
2 tablespoons apricot jam
½ pint/250ml whipping cream
*1 tablespoon Calvados
    (optional)*

Preheat oven to 180°C, 350°F, gas mark 4. Line a 9in/23cm springform tin with baking paper. Beat the eggs and the sugar until thick, pale and creamy. Gently fold in the flour and pour into the tin. Bake until a skewer or fine knife comes out clean. Remove from tin, peel off the baking paper and cool on a wire tray.

Peel, core and chop the apples. Stew gently with the sultanas in water until they form a purée (it does not have to be completely smooth). Stir in the brown sugar and jam and allow to cool.

When both the cake and the filling are cold, whip the cream (combined with the Calvados if you wish) and assemble as follows. Cut the cake in half and spread three-quarters of the filling plus a quarter of the whipped cream on the base. Place the top on gently. Pile the rest of the filling in the middle of the top layer and surround with rosettes of whipped cream.

Marmalade Cake

6oz/175g butter or margarine
6oz/175g soft brown sugar
*Grated rind and juice of one
    orange*
*2 tablespoons thick-cut
    marmalade*
3 eggs, well beaten
8oz/225g self-raising flour
1 teaspoon ground mixed spice
3oz/75g mixed dried fruit
2 tablespoons milk

ICING
6oz/175g icing sugar
*Grated rind and juice of ½ an
    orange*
*2 teaspoons marmalade (non-
    chunky if possible)*

Preheat oven to 180°C, 350°F, gas mark 4. Line a 9in/23cm round, loose-based cake tin with baking paper or well-greased greaseproof. Cream together the butter or margarine, brown sugar, orange rind and juice and marmalade. Beat in the eggs. Sift the flour and spice together and fold in to the mixture together with the dried fruit and the milk. When you have a smooth consistency, transfer the mixture to the tin. Smooth the top. Cover the top with greaseproof paper to prevent it scorching. Bake for approx. 1¼ to 1½ hours. Remove from tin and cool the cake on a wire tray.

To finish the cake, mix the icing sugar in a bowl with the juice and the runny marmalade. Spoon on to the top of the cake. You will find it almost spreads itself. Use the grated orange rind to decorate the cake with a central rosette and a ring on top of the icing.

Honey Bread

5oz/150g soft brown sugar
2 tablespoons honey
¼ pint/150ml hot milk
9oz/250g self-raising flour
¼ pint/150ml cold milk

Preheat oven to 180°C, 350°F, gas mark 4. Grease and flour or line with baking paper a 1lb/450g loaf tin. In a mixing bowl beat the sugar, honey and hot milk together until well blended. Sift in self-raising flour and add cold milk. Beat again until smooth. Put mixture into tin, smooth the top and bake for about an hour, until golden.

Welsh Cakes

1lb/450g self-raising flour
Pinch salt
½ teaspoon mixed spice
3oz/75g butter or margarine
3oz/75g lard
6oz/175g sugar
2oz/50g currants
1 egg
3 tablespoons milk

Sift together the flour, salt and spice. Rub in the butter or margarine and lard. Then add the sugar and currants. Beat the egg with the milk and use to bind the mixture to a soft dough. Roll out and cut into circles or triangles. Bake on a griddle or in a heavy-based frying-pan for approx. 7 to 8 minutes on each side. Serve warm with butter.

In the Welsh language, Welsh cakes are *Pice ar y Maen*. They are very similar to Northumberland's Singin' Hinnies (p.122), but richer and slightly spicier.

ST MICHAEL'S MOUNT
CORNWALL

The first view of St Michael's Mount is breathtaking. The castle and church appear to rise sheer from the sea. It is easy to believe the many myths and stories which surround this rocky island just off the far south-western tip of Cornwall.

In turn it has been religious foundation, fortress and much-loved family home. Each succeeding use of the island has left traces for visitors to discover as they climb the steep paths and steps which lead up to and through the castle. The keep itself is part medieval, part Victorian, though I defy anyone to see where the old castle stops and the new one begins. The church and the Chevy Chase Room are oldest survivals from the medieval priory, the entrance hall and the armoury are sixteenth-century and the elegant blue drawing-rooms are eighteenth-century.

To reach the island at high tide you must take a short boat trip, at low tide you can walk across a stone causeway. Henry V, victor at Agincourt, took possession of the Benedictine priory on the Mount from the French in 1425. The prior started building the harbour and the causeway using the men of Marazion, the village on the mainland opposite as labour, but ran into what today is called 'a cash-flow crisis'. This problem was solved by the Bishop of Exeter granting an indulgence to anyone who repented of his sins and contributed to the cost of building. So the causeway was paid for from the sins of Cornishmen!

Whatever its role, as place of pilgrimage, fortress or home, the inhabitants of the Mount have always formed a close-knit community and still do. They have to be. The weather still rules here. If the sea is too rough the ferry boats cannot run and the Mount may be cut off from the outside world.

Among the buildings that line the little harbour and house today's small hamlet of island administration, two shops, the information centre and the café you will find the Sail Loft Restaurant. The difficulties of running a restaurant on an island are balanced by a wonderful supply of fresh fish and the joy of working in such a special place. If you are lucky enough to be nearby in Cornwall, do go. The myths and stories are right, the Mount is magical.

Hobbler's Seafood Pie

12oz/350g white fish (the Sea Loft uses ling for preference, but cod or haddock may be easier to find)
4oz/125g peeled prawns
1 tablespoon chopped parsley
2oz/50g butter
2oz/50g flour
½ pint/250ml creamy milk
½ pint/250ml fish stock
1lb/450g mashed potato

Preheat oven to 180°C, 350°F, gas mark 4. Cut the fish into large chunks and lay it on the bottom of a pie dish. Scatter over the prawns and the parsley. Make up a thick white sauce using the butter, flour, milk and fish stock and pour over the fish. Cover the fish and sauce with mashed potato, fluffing the top with a fork. Bake uncovered in the oven for approx. 30 minutes, until the top is crisp and brown.

Using raw fish seems to intensify the flavour. At the Sea Loft this pie is made with any fish the boats land on the Mount, so generally there are leftovers after filleting for the stock, but if you buy fish from the supermarket it will probably be easier to use a vegetable stock cube.

West Country Honeyed Pork Stew

1 tablespoon vegetable oil
1 lb/450 g shoulder of pork, diced
2 oz/50 g butter-beans
1 medium onion stuck with cloves
1 teaspoon mixed herbs
1 tablespoon clear honey
1 pint/500 ml chicken stock
½ pint/250 ml apple juice
3 medium carrots, peeled and cut into 1½ in/3 cm sticks
2 sticks of celery, chopped
2 leeks, washed and chopped
2 tablespoons Worcestershire sauce
1 tablespoon tomato purée
Salt and pepper to taste

You will need to start this recipe the day before you cook it by soaking the butter-beans.

Heat the vegetable oil in an ovenproof casserole and sauté the pork until nicely browned. Drain the beans and add to the pork together with the onion and mixed herbs. Turn everything for a minute or two in the oil. Then add honey, stock and apple juice. Bring to the boil, reduce the heat, cover the pan and simmer for approx. an hour, until the beans are just becoming tender. Add carrots, celery, leeks, Worcestershire sauce and tomato purée. Simmer a further 30 minutes, or until the meat is tender and the vegetables are cooked.

Peppers with a Spicy Lentil Stuffing

4 large peppers, preferably different colours
8 oz/225 g red lentils
3 tablespoons olive oil
1 large mild onion
½ teaspoon ground cumin
½ teaspoon ground coriander
½ teaspoon mixed herbs
1 tablespoons tomato purée
½ pint/250 ml béchamel sauce (optional)

Preheat oven to 190°C, 375°F, gas mark 5. Cut the peppers in half, de-pip them and poach them for 5 minutes in boiling water. Drain and arrange in alternating colours in an oven-proof dish. Put the lentils in a saucepan, cover with water and cook until soft and the water is absorbed. This takes approx. 20 minutes. Heat one tablespoon of the olive oil, sauté the onion with the cumin, coriander and herbs until soft. Remove from the heat and stir in the tomato purée and the lentils. Use this mixture to stuff the pepper halves. Dribble the rest of the olive oil over the top of the peppers and cook uncovered in the oven for 20 minutes.

If the peppers are an accompaniment to a meat dish, they need nothing further, but if they are to be served as a vegetarian main dish with rice or potatoes, then accompany them with a creamy white sauce served separately.

Steamed Ginger Sponge Pudding

4oz/125g butter
4oz/125g caster sugar
2 eggs
6oz/175g self-raising flour
2oz/50g stem ginger, finely
   chopped
3 tablespoons syrup

Butter a 1½ pint/900ml pudding basin. Cream together butter and sugar until pale and fluffy. Beat in the eggs, adding one spoon of flour with each egg. Fold in the flour and the chopped ginger. Spoon the syrup into the bottom of the pudding basin, then the pudding mixture on top. Smooth the top. Cover with a layer of greaseproof paper and foil and steam for 1 to 1½ hours.

While the pudding is steaming, make the Ginger Sauce (below). Turn the pudding out and serve the sauce separately. Serve both warm – there is no need to burn tongues, the gentle spiciness will add its own heat.

Ginger Sauce

1 tablespoon fresh ginger,
   grated
½ pint/250ml full cream milk
1oz/25g butter
1oz/25g plain flour
2oz/50g caster sugar

Bring the milk to the boil with the ginger. Let the mixture stand for at least 30 minutes to infuse. Then strain off the milk. Melt the butter slowly and stir in the flour, cook gently for 2 to 3 minutes, add the milk gradually, stirring all the time. Bring the sauce to the boil and allow to simmer for at least 5 minutes, stirring constantly. Add the sugar and stir until it is dissolved.

Lemon Geranium Syllabub

8 lemon geranium leaves
Juice of 1 lemon
6 tablespoons white wine
3 tablespoons caster sugar
½ pint/250ml thick double
   cream
Zest of lemon and fresh lemon
   geranium leaves to garnish

Bruise the lemon geranium leaves and infuse them in the lemon juice, white wine and sugar. Chill for at least 30 minutes in the fridge (if the infusion is very cold it will whisk more easily with the cream). Discard the leaves and stir the cream into the infusion. Whisk until thick; this can take some time, it depends on the weather! If it is hot and thundery, whisk gently and gradually to prevent the mixture curdling. When thick, pile into glasses and decorate with lemon zest and lemon geranium leaves.

This is the most delectable flowery syllabub.

SALTRAM
DEVON

On the banks of the River Plym in South Devon, set in the centre of a landscaped park, stands Saltram, a dove-grey stucco mansion. Saltram's heyday was the late eighteenth century. Wars with America, France and Spain drew many distinguished figures from the highest society to Plymouth. Saltram's convenient location and its ability to lodge important visitors in appropriate style made it one of the grandest houses in the West Country.

Today a visit to Saltram is a step back into that elegant world. It was largely created by two generations of remarkable women. Lady Catherine Parker built this house in the mid-eighteenth century around an older Tudor building. It is very much her house: no architect is mentioned and tradition says she herself supervised the building. Her portrait by Thomas Hudson which hangs in the hall shows a handsome, commanding woman with a calm decisive gaze. Dressed in the height of fashion and wearing a dashing feathered hat, she looks across at her son John Parker whose second wife, Theresa Robinson, was the other woman whose choices in decoration, furniture and pictures we still see today.

Theresa married John in 1769, the year after he inherited the estate. John was a rich country gentleman with a grand house, but Saltram was a long way from polite society. Theresa came from a worldly and cultured background: her father was British Ambassador in Vienna when she was born, and the Empress Maria Theresa stood as her godmother, hence her Christian name. She set about transforming Saltram, landscaping the grounds and building a summer-house and an orangery to enhance them. She commissioned Robert Adam to design a grand saloon and library. Adam liked to plan and draw everything, including the carpet, the pelmets, the mirrors. The library is now the Dining Room but the sumptuous Saloon is still a perfect Adam masterpiece down to the door knobs.

Theresa commissioned and collected pictures by Angelica Kauffmann and Sir Joshua Reynolds, amongst others. Reynolds, who was born in the neighbouring parish of Plympton, was a life-long friend of John Parker and painted a picture of Theresa in a classically elegant pose, which now hangs in the Saloon. Sadly Theresa was only to live six years at Saltram, dying a few weeks after the birth of her daughter in 1775. John Parker was heartbroken, and he never remarried. Her sister Anne moved in to look after little Theresa and her older brother Jack, running the household until John died in 1788.

During Anne Robinson's reign, the Great Kitchen was built after a fire in 1778. It is a wonderful room complete with open range and every kind of kitchen utensil. Six hundred copper pans and moulds line the walls. Cockroach catchers are a salutary reminder of a less hygienic age.

An earlier, Tudor kitchen is now the restaurant. It is homely and welcoming with stone flags on the floor and a large dresser on which appetising cakes are displayed. Local crab is a speciality so I am delighted to have an excellent recipe for that very English delicacy, Potted Crab.

Potted Crab

2 tablespoons dry or medium
   sherry
Juice and rind of 1 orange
   (retain 1 teaspoon of the zest
   to use in the clarified butter)
5 oz/150 g butter
8 oz/225 g dressed crab (white
   and dark meat)
¼ teaspoon ground ginger
Salt and pepper
2 oz/50 g butter
2 tablespoons water

Bring sherry, orange rind, and juice to the boil and boil hard until reduced to 1 tablespoon of liquid. Remove from the heat, cool and beat with softened butter until creamy. Combine with the crab meat and ginger. Add salt and pepper to taste. Mix well and spoon into ramekins. Seal with orange clarified butter made as follows.

Bring 1 teaspoon zest of orange, 2 oz/50 g of butter and 2 tablespoons of water slowly to the boil. Remove from heat, allow to cool slightly and gently spoon over the ramekins.

Chill in the refrigerator for at least a couple of hours. Serve with hot toast or melba toast. Potted crab keeps well for two or three days in the fridge.

Chicken and Ham Pie

8 oz/225 g cooked chicken meat
8 oz/225 g cooked ham
4 oz/250 g fresh breadcrumbs
½ small onion, peeled and finely
   chopped
1 stick of celery, finely chopped
1 teaspoon mixed herbs
Zest of 1 lemon
Salt and pepper
1 egg
2 oz/50 g butter
2 oz/50 g flour
½ pint/250 ml chicken, ham or
   vegetable stock
½ pint/250 ml creamy milk
1 tablespoon chopped parsley

SHORTCRUST PASTRY
8 oz/225 g plain flour
4 oz/125 g margarine or lard
Egg and milk glaze
2 oz/50 g sesame seeds

Preheat oven to 190°C, 375°F, gas mark 5. Cut the chicken and ham into chunks. Mix together the breadcrumbs, chopped onion and celery, herbs, lemon zest and salt and pepper to taste. Use the egg to bind into a dryish stuffing. Form the stuffing into balls the size of a large marble. Mix together the chicken, ham and stuffing balls and use to fill a deep pie dish.

Make a white sauce with the butter, flour, stock and milk and stir in the parsley. Season with salt and pepper and pour over the pie filling.

Roll out the pastry and cover the dish, using any trimmings as decoration. Brush with egg glaze and cover with a layer of sesame seeds. Bake 30 to 40 minutes, until golden brown.

SOUTER LIGHTHOUSE
TYNE AND WEAR

Between the industrialised rivers of the Tyne and the Wear stretches a windswept coast of limestone cliffs, grassland and beach. In good weather the beaches and cliffs provide a welcome break from city life for Tynesiders. On bad days, when the wind howls and the waves crash against Lot's Wife, Jack Rock and Pompey's Wife, the forbidding rock stacks which loom in the bay, and the air is misty with spume and spray, it is immensely reassuring to glimpse the bright red-and-white tower of Souter Lighthouse standing high above the largest stack of all, Marsden Rock, on grassy Lizard Point.

During the nineteenth century, the north-eastern coastal traffic increased dramatically and with it the shipwrecks. During 1869 alone twenty vessels came to grief on this stretch of coast. The lighthouse at Souter was designed by James Douglass, one of a distinguished family of lighthousemen, and opened as a matter of urgency in 1871.

Douglass's design was a world-beater: '... no lighthouse in any part of the world would bear comparison with it', boasted the Deputy-Master of Trinity House at Souter's opening. At that time, the Souter light was one of the most technologically advanced, the first to be powered by electrical alternators. Douglass's system of turntable and prisms ensured a light of maximum efficiency. For the next hundred years seamen used its powerful beam to steer away from the dangerous submerged rocks in Sunderland Bay.

A qualified engineer and four assistant keepers ran the lighthouse. It was a 24-hour job, so of course their families lived here too. Within the whitewashed buildings at the foot of the tower is a delightful reconstruction of a keeper's cottage. The tea set out in the kitchen ready for his return from shift brings the close world of this little community vividly to life. The heart was the engine room and the light itself. A tour, with one of the knowledgeable volunteers explaining how it all worked, is a fascinating glimpse into an important facet of our maritime past.

Over the years, the engines in the engine room changed, the light was brought up to date, the fuel changed to oil and then back to electricity and, finally, in 1988 the light was extinguished for the last time. I was delighted to discover, however, that the lighthouse is not simply a record of past times. It is still making a positive contribution to navigation as an automatic radio beacon.

A new lively community of enthusiasts polish the beautiful machinery and explain the fascinating mechanisms to visitors. A popular local birthday treat for lucky children is a trip to Souter and a slice of chocolate cake served in the cosy little rooms of the restaurant converted from one of the keeper's cottages.

Vegetable Barley Broth

2 pints/1250ml strong vegetable
   stock
1oz/25g pearl barley
1oz/25g red lentils
1 carrot, peeled and grated
1 onion, peeled and chopped
   fine
1 leek, chopped fine
½ medium turnip, peeled and
   grated
1 stick of celery, chopped fine
½ red pepper chopped fine
Parsley and grated hard cheese
   to garnish

Put everything in a large saucepan, bring the mixture to the boil, then simmer for at least an hour. Everything should be well cooked and the flavour of the mixed vegetables brought out. Serve piping hot, sprinked with chopped parsley and grated cheese, allowing a large bowl per person.

This is a main course soup, traditional fare to keep out the cold winds from the North Sea. At Souter, regulars visit time and time again for this soup. I was told: 'You should be able to stand your spoon up in it.'

Leek and Onion Scones

1 tablespoon olive oil
1 leek, cleaned and chopped fine
1 small onion, chopped fine
Pinch of sugar
1lb/450g self-raising flour
Salt to taste
4oz/125g butter
½ pint/250ml milk

Preheat oven to 230°C, 450°F, gas mark 8. Either grease a baking sheet or line it with baking paper. Heat oil and sauté the chopped leek and onion with the pinch of sugar until soft. Sift flour with salt and rub in the butter until the mixture resembles fine breadcrumbs. Stir in the leek and onion and sufficient milk to form a soft dough. Turn out on to a floured surface and knead lightly. Roll out to approx. ½in/1cm thick. Stamp out 2in/5cm rounds. Place on baking sheet and brush tops with milk. Bake for approx. 12 minutes, or until golden brown.

Served with both soup and cheese at Souter – and equally good with either.

Singin' Hinnies

8 oz/225 g plain flour
2 oz/50 g butter
2 oz/50 g lard
1 oz/25 g currants
1 teaspoon baking powder
½ teaspoon salt
Milk and soured cream to mix

Preheat oven to 180°C, 350°F, gas mark 4. In a mixing bowl large enough to take all the ingredients, rub the fats into the flour. Add the other dry ingredients. Mix to a soft dough with the milk and soured cream. Roll out and cut into rounds the size of a muffin, about 1 in/2.5 cm thick.

Traditionally, Singin' Hinnies are cooked on a griddle or in a heavy-based frying-pan. You can also bake them in an oven. Allow about 15 minutes in all, turning and flattening them after 7 to 8 minutes. Serve warm, split and buttered.

Singin' Hinnies are a local Northumbrian delicacy. 'Hinnie' is a term of endearment, used especially for children. The fat in the Hinnies makes them 'sing' when they are cooking. They are ready to eat when the singing stops. Impatient children would be told to wait for their tea, 'it's still singin' Hinnie'.

Souter Chocolate Cake

7 oz/200 g self-raising flour
8 oz/225 g caster sugar
Pinch of salt
1 oz/25 g cocoa
4 oz/125 g margarine
3 eggs beaten with 3 fl oz/75 ml evaporated milk
A few drops of vanilla essence

ICING
2½ oz/60 g butter
1 oz/25 g cocoa
4 oz/125 g icing sugar
3 tablespoons/45 ml hot milk
A few drops of vanilla essence

Preheat oven to 180°C, 350°F, gas mark 4. Line either an 8 in/20cm diameter deep cake tin or two sandwich tins with baking paper. Sieve together the flour, sugar, salt and cocoa. Rub in the margarine until the mixture resembles coarse breadcrumbs. Stir in the eggs and milk and the vanilla essence and beat well for 5 minutes. Fill the tin or tins and bake for approx. 30 minutes if using sandwich tins or for an hour for the deep cake, or until a skewer comes out of the centre clean. Allow to cool completely on a wire rack before icing.

Melt the butter in a saucepan, stir in the cocoa and cook gently for a couple of minutes. Then remove from the heat, stir in the icing sugar, milk and vanilla essence. Beat well until the mixture is smooth and thick. Spread on the cake with a palette knife and allow to rest until set.

STANDEN
WEST SUSSEX

Standen is the fortunate result of an unusually harmonious partnership between architect and client. James Beale, a successful Victorian lawyer, wanted a comfortable country house so he and his large family could enjoy an active life away from the city. Philip Webb's speciality was designing houses which drew on tradition but used modern ideas to make them work beautifully for the people who lived in them. Unusual among architects, he also had the reputation for keeping to budget. 'The whole of the work is to be done with the *best* materials and workmanship of their several kinds . . .'. This sentence from Webb's specification for Standen in 1891 can stand as a description of what we see now.

The interior is a treasure house of the Arts and Crafts movement. Webb himself designed all the many and varied chimneypieces, every detail of the panelling, delicate light fittings (using newly available electricity, of course), the dressers, wardrobes and shelving. His friend William Morris supplied carpets, wallpapers and fabrics, even furniture. Exquisite Della Robbia and William de Morgan pottery pieces glow on the shelves. Brass beds are by Heal & Co., other items came from Messrs Liberty.

Standen is no dry as dust museum though. Wandering through the large light rooms, the scented conservatory and the delightful garden, it is easy to imagine the Beale family, children, grandchildren and friends enjoying each other's company; conversation and games of billiards inside, promenades and croquet outdoors. Standen now invites visitors to pause and enjoy the atmosphere of a house and garden from a slower, more leisured age.

Turn sharp left by the gate and you will find yourself in an ancient timbered barn. Webb was a founder member of the Society for the Protection of Ancient Buildings and concerned for natural features. The barn is part of a group of much older buildings which he incorporated into the new house. It is now the restaurant. James Beale's sister-in-law, Mary, a famous cook in her day and the author of the hugely popular *Wholesome Cookery* published in 1886, would have approved of the recipes for Fresh Tomato Soup and Shepherd's Pie which continue the Standen tradition of good home cooking using excellent local ingredients.

Fresh Tomato Soup

2oz/50g butter
2 garlic cloves, crushed
1 medium onion, chopped
1 small potato, peeled and
  chopped
1lb/450g tomatoes, roughly
  chopped
1 bay leaf
2 tablespoons tomato purée
¾ pint/400ml vegetable stock
¾ pint/400ml milk
Salt and freshly ground black
  pepper

Melt the butter in a saucepan and sauté the onion together with the crushed garlic cloves until they are soft but not coloured. Add the potato, tomatoes, bay leaf, tomato purée and stock. Cover and simmer for 20 minutes. Take off the heat, stir in the milk and remove the bay leaf. Blend until smooth, season with salt and pepper to taste. Reheat to just below boiling to serve.

Shepherd's Pie

1oz/25g butter or margarine
1 large onion, finely chopped
2 carrots, peeled and finely
    chopped
1lb/450g minced lamb
1 tablespoon flour
½ pint/250ml beef or lamb
    stock
1 tablespoon tomato purée
1 dessertspoon Worcestershire
    sauce
½ teaspoon dried mixed herbs
Salt and freshly ground black
    pepper

TOPPING
1lb/450g potato, peeled and
    sliced
1oz/25g butter
¼ pint/150ml half cream or
    1 large egg, well beaten

Preheat oven to 190°C, 375°F, gas mark 5. Melt the butter or margarine in a saucepan and sauté the onion and chopped carrots until the onion is soft but not coloured. Add the minced lamb and cook gently until the meat is browned. Stir in flour and cook for 5 minutes. Gradually stir in stock, tomato purée, Worcestershire sauce, herbs and seasoning and bring to the boil. Reduce the heat, cover the pan and simmer for 15 minutes. Turn into an ovenproof dish and allow to cool a little before topping with potato.

Boil potatoes and drain. Mash them and beat in butter, together with cream or egg. Season to taste with salt and pepper. Pipe or spread the potato with a fork over the meat. Bake for 20 to 30 minutes, until the top is golden brown.

This well-loved recipe can be made with beef mince, in which case it is called Cottage Pie.

Pasta, Grape and Seed Salad with Blue Cheese Dressing

14oz/400g tricolore pasta
    spirals
4oz/125g black grapes
1oz/25g sunflower seeds
1oz/25g pumpkin seeds
2 tablespoons parsley,
    chopped fine

DRESSING
2oz/50g blue cheese
5fl oz/125ml fromage frais
2 tablespoons single cream
Black pepper to taste

Cook the pasta as directed on the packet in plenty of boiling salted water. Drain and rinse immediately in cold water. Pip the grapes. Blend the blue cheese with the fromage frais and cream, season with black pepper (it should not need salt). Pour over the pasta. Add the grapes, sunflower and pumpkin seeds and 1 tablespoon of the parsley to the pasta and mix well to coat all the ingredients. Transfer to a salad bowl and sprinkle the top with the rest of the parsley.

STOWE LANDSCAPE GARDENS
BUCKINGHAMSHIRE

'Our England is a garden that is full of stately views.' The first line of Kipling's poem 'The Glory of the Garden' is a perfect description of Stowe, arguably the most important landscape garden in Britain.

Throughout the eighteenth century, the Temple family created an idealised classical landscape which at its peak comprised an enormous 10,000 acres. Today it still takes stout shoes and a couple of hours to do a complete tour of the 1,200 or so acres of gardens and park that are in the Trust's care.

Don't worry though, if your visit has to be shorter. Every 'stately view' at Stowe is a revelation. The harmonious combination of the natural, grassy vistas, informal groups of trees and water is everywhere complemented by the man-made. The Temple family's motto 'How delightful are thy temples' is brought triumphantly to life with a rich variety of monuments, statuary and follies, all placed in the garden to give maximum delight to the eye. The changeable English climate suits Stowe beautifully. On a wet day other walkers are few. The views are subtle and mysterious. Every misty avenue invites exploration, the statues and temples seem almost dream-like.

In brilliant sun, the water on the lake sparkles, the pale green grass and the deeper green of the trees set off the golden stone of the monuments with diamond clarity. It is easy to picture Stowe in its heyday. In 1805, Betsey Wynne, a cousin of the Duke of Buckingham, then Stowe's owner, recorded that up to 10,000 visitors attended a *fête champêtre* here; complete with two royal princes, masquers, 'groupes of Morice Dancers, the Bands of the Pandeons, Savoyards and of the Regiments who were on the water', fireworks and special illumination of the Grotto, the Bridge and the Obelisk. 'Nothing could exceed the splendour and magnificence of the Dining room especially when the candles were lighted.' Betsey was very impressed by the setting for dinner with the royal princes, but we do not know whether she enjoyed the food, for she did not comment.

Nowadays you will find tasty soups, generously filled rolls and seductive homemade cakes available either in the open air or in temporary accommodation behind the Temple of Concord and Victory.

Vegetable Soups

VEGETABLE PURÉE BASE
1 tablespoon sunflower oil
1 medium onion, finely chopped
1lb/450g potatoes
1 pint/500ml vegetable stock

This is a particularly good idea: a potato and onion purée base which is used to create soups suitable for different seasons.

Sauté the onion gently in the oil in a large saucepan until it is soft but not coloured. Add the potatoes, peeled and roughly chopped, and the vegetable stock. Bring the mixture to the boil, reduce the heat and simmer until the potato is cooked. Purée the mixture. It is now ready to be transformed into:

CARROT AND CARAWAY SOUP

1 pint/500ml milk
1 teaspoon caraway seeds
2 medium carrots, peeled and grated
Salt and pepper to taste

In a separate pan bring the milk to the boil with the caraway seeds. Turn off the heat and allow it to stand and the seeds to infuse the milk. Strain off the seeds, add the milk and the grated carrot to the vegetable purée (see above). Stir and cook gently until the carrot is cooked but still crunchy. Season with salt and pepper to taste. Serve with a few caraway seeds scattered on the top.

Early spring carrots with their fresh, sweet flavour are particularly suitable.

BROCCOLI AND STILTON SOUP

1 pint/500ml milk
1 head of broccoli
2oz/50g cubed Stilton
Salt and pepper to taste

Divide the broccoli into florets and cook gently in the milk until soft. It is important not to overcook it as the colour will not be so good. Liquidise the cooked broccoli and add the mixture to the vegetable purée (see above). Add a little more vegetable stock if the mixture is too thick. Bring the soup back to just below boiling, crumble in the Stilton, season if necessary and serve immediately.

This soup is piquant and a beautiful green in colour. Make it after Christmas to use up any leftover Stilton.

PEA AND HAM SOUP

4oz/125g dried split peas
1 pint/500ml chicken stock
2oz/50g smoked German ham,
*   diced*
Chopped parsley to garnish

Soak the peas overnight. Drain and cook in the chicken stock. Liquidise and combine with the purée base (see above). The soup should be very thick but if you prefer a slightly thinner soup, dilute with a little more stock. Bring up to the boil. Add the chopped ham, a little chopped parsley and serve very hot.

Dried split peas and smoked German ham give a thick hearty soup, particularly warming after an invigorating, but cold, winter walk.

ROSEMARY SOUP

1 pint/500ml milk
3in/7.5cm sprig of rosemary
1oz/25g chopped butter
1oz/25g chopped Cheddar
A little extra rosemary to
*   garnish*

In a pan bring the milk up to the boil with the rosemary. Turn off the heat and allow the milk to stand for at least an hour for the milk to be infused. Then discard the rosemary and add the milk to the vegetable purée (see above). Reheat gently to just below boiling. Mix in the butter and cheese and serve immediately with a little chopped rosemary in each soup bowl.

Rosemary soup is breathtakingly simple but gives a subtle, sophisticated creamy soup fit for any dinner party. Make it with the young rosemary leaves of early summer which are especially fragrant. You can vary the amount of rosemary according to taste. I love rosemary and use four sprigs for a strong flavour.

Bread Pudding

¾ pint/400 ml milk
¼ pint/150 ml cold strong tea
4 oz/125 g butter, melted
1 tablespoon mixed spice
3 eggs, well beaten
12 oz/350 g mixed dried fruit
1 lb/450 g fresh breadcrumbs

Either grease a tin 2 in/5 cm deep and 8 in × 11 in/20 cm × 28 cm wide or line it with baking paper. Combine milk, tea, melted butter, mixed spice, beaten eggs and dried fruit and mix well. Mix in the breadcrumbs and leave to soak for at least an hour or overnight if you wish. Spread the mixture into the prepared tin and bake at 180°C, 350°F, gas mark 4 for 1 hour 15 minutes. Cool and serve cut into squares.

Chocolate Caramel Shortbread

SHORTBREAD
12 oz/350 g plain flour
8 oz/225 g butter
4 oz/125 g sugar

CARAMEL
8 oz/225 g butter or margarine
4 oz/125 g caster sugar
1 tablespoon golden syrup
7½ oz/215 g tin condensed milk
6 oz/175 g plain chocolate for
    topping

Preheat oven to 150°C, 300°F, gas mark 2. Line a Swiss roll tin with baking paper. Rub the butter into the flour until the mixture resembles coarse breadcrumbs. Stir in the sugar and form into a soft dough. Either press or roll this into the base of the Swiss roll tin. Smooth the top and bake until golden, approx. 40 minutes.

Place all the ingredients for the caramel into a large saucepan (non-stick if possible) and stir over a low heat until melted. Then bring to the boil and allow to boil steadily until the mixture begins to thicken and go golden. Stir constantly to stop it sticking. Cool a little, then spread it over the shortbread in a thick layer. Leave until set.

When the caramel is set, melt the chocolate in a bowl over boiling water. Use the melted chocolate to cover the caramel and leave until cold. Cut into squares to serve.

My daughter worked in a delicatessen where this was called 'Millionaires' Shortbread'! It is very rich, so make the squares smallish but there is never any waste, everyone loves it and if you *can* save any, it will keep in an airtight tin for months.

Chocolate Cake

8oz/225g self-raising flour
8oz/225g soft brown sugar
4oz/125g ground almonds
2oz/50g cocoa
2 level teaspoons bicarbonate
  of soda
6 eggs, well beaten
8oz/225g soft margarine
4oz/125g golden syrup, mixed
  together with ¼ pint/150ml
  hot water
Jam
Cream or butter icing
Icing sugar

Preheat oven to 160°C, 325°F, gas mark 3. Either grease or line with baking paper a 9in/23cm springform cake tin. Measure self-raising flour, sugar and almonds into a mixing bowl large enough to take all the ingredients. Sieve the cocoa and bicarbonate of soda together – mix for 3 minutes. Add eggs, soft margarine, syrup and water and mix for a further 3 minutes. Pour the mixture into the prepared tin. Bake for 45 minutes to an hour. Remove from the tin and cool on wire tray.

When cold, split and fill with jam and cream or butter icing. Dust the top with icing sugar.

The cocoa and the almonds give a rich, dark, moist cake.

Swiss Carrot Cake

8oz/225g wholemeal flour
2 teaspoons cinnamon
1 teaspoon ground nutmeg
4oz/125g desiccated coconut
4oz/125g mixed dried fruit
4 eggs
8oz/225g soft brown sugar
6fl oz/175ml vegetable oil
8oz/225g carrot, grated

Preheat oven to 180°C, 350°F, gas mark 4. Either grease a 9in/23cm springform tin or line it with baking paper. Sift flour, cinnamon and nutmeg together in a large mixing bowl. Stir in the coconut and dried fruit. Whisk the eggs and sugar until thick and creamy. Stir the oil into the eggs and sugar slowly and mix until blended. Make a well in the flour and other dry ingredients and fold in the creamy mixture alternately with the grated carrot. Transfer the combination to the prepared tin and smooth the top. Bake for approx. an hour or until a skewer pushed into the thickest part of the cake comes out clean. Remove from tin and cool on a wire rack.

This cake is Cranks inspired. The crystallised peel in the mixed fruit gives it a distinctive flavour and the coconut a particular texture. It is nutty and moist and tastes even better a day or two after baking.

SUTTON HOUSE
LONDON

Sutton House is one of the National Trust's most unusual properties, with a thoroughly chequered past and a very lively present.

In the sixteenth century, Hackney was a small village three miles from the City of London, noted for its 'healthful air'. Just the place for the ambitious and successful courtier Ralph Sadleir to build in 1534 the 'bryk place', the brick-built Tudor mansion that lies at the heart of today's house. Sadleir, a 'man on the make', predictably sold the house in 1550 and moved on to an even grander mansion in Hertfordshire.

During the next century the house had several owners, including James I's

Master of the Rolls, memorably named Julius Caesar. In 1670 it was leased by Mrs Sarah Freeman as a girls' school. By this time Hackney was a genteel suburb so full of schools it was known as 'The Ladies' University of Female Arts'. Contemporary commentators differed in their opinions on the education the young ladies received. Samuel Pepys, always susceptible to feminine charm, found the girls 'very pretty'. John Aubrey, more sternly, condemned the schools as places 'where young maids learnt pride and wantonness'. Sutton House was divided into two, around 1750, and was then further subdivided with private dwellings side by side with schools.

By 1890 Hackney was very much part of London. Factories along the Lee Navigation necessitated more lower-class housing for workers. Better transport led the middle classes to move to greener sites further out of town. Sutton House was again united and became St John's Institute, a recreational centre for working men, with social, writing, billiard and committee rooms, a library and a hostel. The centre was such a success that in 1936 it outgrew Sutton House and moved out. From 1938 the house was owned, but leased out, by the National Trust. This was its darkest hour. It only just survived the bombs of the Second World War, a variety of tenants, squatters, thieves, vandals and the attention of developers. Fortunately, a pressure group of local residents, Save Sutton House, came to its rescue, in 1988 persuading the Trust to organise its repair and refurbishment.

Now Sutton House is a focal point for the discovery of the past of Hackney, as well as celebrating its present and future. The work of local artists is displayed in the gallery; concerts and functions are held in the Wenlock Barn. Visitors can tour the beautiful Tudor panelled rooms at the heart of the building and study the story of the oldest surviving family house in East London.

Part of the latest refurbishment is Grumbolds, a delightful, conservatory-style restaurant. Hackney is renowned for its ethnic mix and the diverse and delicious food at Grumbolds reflects this.

Spicy Marinaded Chicken with Yoghurt and Cucumber Dressing

4 × 6 oz/4 × 175 g *chicken breasts*
  in 1 in/2 cm pieces
2 *cloves garlic, finely chopped*
Zest and juice of one lemon
A few sprigs of fresh coriander,
  roughly chopped
1 *teaspoon turmeric*
2 *teaspoons garam masala*
1 *teaspoon cumin*
2 *teaspoons olive oil*
Salt and pepper to taste

DRESSING
½ *pint/250 ml natural yoghurt*
3 oz/75 g *peeled cucumber,*
  grated coarsely or finely diced
1 *tablespoon fresh mint*
Salt and pepper

Mix all the ingredients, except those for the dressing, in a bowl, making sure the chicken is well coated. Cover and refrigerate over night or all day to enable the flavours to permeate the chicken.

Preheat oven to 220°C, 425°F, gas mark 7. Line a baking tray with baking paper, or brush the tray with a little oil. Put the chicken pieces on the tray and cook for approx. 15 minutes. (Try not to overcook as they dry out easily.) While they are cooking, mix together the ingredients for the dressing, adding salt and pepper to taste.

Serve the chicken pieces piled on a bed of saffron rice, spoon over the dressing and serve immediately. Mango chutney and a salad of tomato, onion and cumin seeds complement this dish.

Mushroom and Pepper Biryani

2 oz/50 g *butter*
2 *large onions, finely chopped*
3 *cloves of garlic, finely*
  chopped
1¼ in/4 cm *chunk of ginger,*
  peeled and finely chopped
1 *teaspoon each of garam*
  masala, turmeric, ground
  cumin, crushed green
  cardamoms
1 *red pepper*
1 *green pepper*
8 oz/225 g *button mushrooms*
Salt and pepper to taste
1 *tablespoon wholemeal flour*
¼ *pint/150 ml milk*
2 *tablespoons (optional)*
  yoghurt
Chopped fresh coriander to
  garnish

Melt the butter in a pan large enough to take all the ingredients. Add the onion, garlic and ginger and fry gently until golden brown. Stir in the spices and cook gently while you de-seed the peppers, cut them into chunky strips and add them to the mixture. Cook a few minutes more until the peppers begin to soften, then add the mushrooms and continue to cook gently for 5 to 10 minutes. The mixture should now be quite juicy. Add the flour and stir well to coat the vegetables. Bring the mixture gently to boiling and simmer for a few minutes to cook the flour. Then add the milk, stirring the mixture as the sauce thickens. Simmer for a minute or two, then remove from the heat and serve immediately. This is the moment to stir in the yoghurt if you prefer a creamier texture, but don't let the mixture boil if you reheat it, as it will curdle.

Serve on a bed of saffron rice, garnished with chopped fresh coriander.

Bean and Cashew Indienne

4oz/125g kidney beans
4oz/125g chick-peas
1 tablespoon sunflower oil
1 small onion, finely diced
1 clove garlic, chopped
1 red pepper, de-seeded and
    chopped
2 pinches mixed spice
2 pinches Madras curry powder
½ pint/250ml apple juice
½ pint/250ml vegetable stock
1 tablespoon tomato purée
1 eating apple, peeled, cored
    and sliced
2oz/50g toasted cashew nuts
1 dessertspoon chopped
    coriander

GARNISH
More fresh coriander
4 tablespoons cream (optional)

This recipe must be started the previous day. Soak beans and chick-peas in water overnight.

The next day, drain and put them in new water. Bring up to boiling and boil hard for 10 minutes. Reduce heat and simmer until cooked, approx. 1 hour. Meanwhile, sauté the onion in the oil for 5 minutes, then add garlic, pepper, mixed spice and curry powder and cook for a further 5 minutes. Add apple juice, stock and tomato purée and simmer for 10 minutes until the sauce has reduced and thickened slightly. Add the beans and chick-peas, sliced apple, toasted cashews and chopped coriander. Stir well and check seasoning. Simmer for 10 minutes. Serve piping hot with rice, garnished with more chopped coriander and an optional swirl of cream.

Sweet Potato Bake

1lb/450g sweet potatoes
4oz/125g mozzarella cheese,
    grated
4oz/125g Cheddar cheese,
    grated
2 eggs
2fl oz/60ml milk
2oz/50g demerara sugar
1oz/25g cinnamon

Preheat oven to 190°C, 375°F, gas mark 5. Peel and dice the sweet potatoes. Boil until tender, but be careful not to over-cook them. Drain and place in a well-greased flan dish. Sprinkle first with the cinnamon and then the two grated cheeses. Mix the eggs with the milk and pour on top. Sprinkle with sugar and place in oven. Bake for 20 to 30 minutes until the top is golden brown.

Savoury Pumpkin Flan

PASTRY
4oz/125g butter or margarine
4oz/125g plain flour
4oz/125g oats
1 egg
2fl oz/60ml milk

FILLING
8oz/225g pumpkin, peeled and
*   chopped*
4oz/125g onion
1oz/25g mixed herbs
4oz/125g Cheddar cheese,
*   grated*
4fl oz/125ml single cream
2 eggs, well beaten
Salt and pepper to taste

Preheat oven to 180°C, 350°F, gas mark 4. Rub the butter or margarine into the flour. Stir in the oats. Mix the egg and milk together and add to the mixture to bind it into a dough. Wrap the pastry in cling film and chill while assembling the filling.

Peel the pumpkin and cook until soft. Drain and liquidise, leave to cool. Finely chop the onion and mix with the pumpkin, mixed herbs, cheese, cream and beaten eggs. Season with salt and pepper to taste.

Roll out the pastry to line a 9in/22cm diameter flan dish. Prick the bottom and add the pumpkin filling. Bake for 30 to 40 minutes.

The next recipe is very similar except that it is a dessert. Pumpkin is more important for texture than taste. It's what you add to it that determines whether it is sweet or savoury.

Sweet Pumpkin Tart

PASTRY
4oz/125g butter or margarine
4oz/125g plain flour
4oz/125g oats
1 egg
2fl oz/60ml milk

FILLING
8oz/225g pumpkin, peeled and
*   chopped*
6fl oz/175ml single cream
3 eggs, well beaten
1oz/25g cinnamon
Pinch of mixed spice
1 teaspoon vanilla essence
4oz/125g caster sugar

Preheat oven to 180°C, 350°F, gas mark 4. Rub the butter or margarine into the flour. Stir in the oats. Mix the egg and milk together and add to the mixture to make a dough. Wrap in cling film and chill while you are mixing the filling.

Peel the pumpkin, dice and boil until soft. Drain and liquidise. Allow to cool. When cool, mix with single cream, eggs, cinnamon, mixed spice, vanilla and sugar. Retain a little sugar to sprinkle on the top of the tart.

Roll out the pastry to line a 9in/22cm flan tin and add the filling. Sprinkle the top with a little sugar.

This flan is spicy but not sweet. A pumpkin flan or pie is a traditional pudding at Thanksgiving after the roast turkey.

TRERICE
CORNWALL

To reach Trerice from the busy A30 you must twist and turn through the narrow Cornish lanes, and even then it is easy to miss. The buildings lie snug in a peaceful valley a few miles inland from Newquay. The house was built by Sir John Arundell in 1573 in the local limestone, now mellowed to a silvery grey, a colour which perfectly complements the elegant curving gables of the east front. Harmoniously in proportion, Trerice is not a grand house; rather it conveys an atmosphere of continuity. A succession of absentee owners in the eighteenth and nineteenth centuries meant that Trerice escaped refurbishment and the core of the house has not been materially altered since the late sixteenth century.

The heart of the house is the Great Chamber. It is a wonderful, light room. Soft West Country sun floods in through the great semicircular window illuminating the rich plasterwork which is the glory of Trerice. Fine plaster friezes, strapwork and decoration can also be seen in the Great Hall. Even the corridors are decorated.

Trerice is furnished with pictures, china and furniture associated with its history and that of the Arundell and Acland families (see p.81) who owned it for four centuries.

Do leave enough time to enjoy a walk in the sheltered walled gardens. Tender plants flourish here in the mild Cornish climate and old varieties of apples and pears are being nurtured in the orchard. The house is part of a group of buildings which includes to the west, The Great Barn. In 1940, during the dark days of the Second World War, when invasion seemed imminent, a renowned battalion of the local Home Guard called 'The Choughs' drilled on the lawn.

Happily the invasion never came and the Home Guard was disbanded. Now The Great Barn is the restaurant where you can drink the local cider and enjoy good Cornish cooking. I was thrilled to be given a recipe for Fairings, delicious crisp ginger biscuits that I had enjoyed in Cornwall since childhood and delighted to find they tasted just as good cooked at home.

Fish Flan

8 oz/225 g shortcrust pastry
1¼ lb/550 g cod fillet
1 pint/500 ml creamy milk
2 oz/50 g peeled prawns
2 oz/50 g butter
2 tablespoons flour
1 teaspoon Dijon mustard

TOPPING
1 oz/25 g brown breadcrumbs
1 oz/25 g Cheddar cheese
1 tablespoon finely chopped
  parsley

Preheat oven to 200°C, 400°F, gas mark 6. Roll out the pastry and line a 9 in/23 cm white quiche dish. Prick the base and bake approx. 15 minutes until the pastry is a light brown and the base feels set and crisp to the touch. Poach the fish in the milk. Drain, reserving the milk. Flake the fish and use to fill the pastry case, scattering on the prawns at the same time. Make a thickish béchamel sauce using the butter, flour, Dijon mustard and milk and spoon this over the fish. Mix the crumbs, cheese and parsley and cover the flan with a thick layer. Return to the oven and bake for approx. 20 minutes, until the top is brown and crisp.

Delicious served with a cucumber and tomato salad.

Mushroom Salad

1 lb/450g button mushrooms
4 tablespoons olive oil
1 large mild onion, peeled and
  chopped
2 cloves garlic, finely chopped
1 tablespoon mixed fresh herbs
  or 1 teaspoon mixed dried
  herbs
1 tablespoon tomato purée
1 dessertspoon white wine
  vinegar
1 tablespoon white wine
Dash of Worcestershire sauce
1 tablespoon mixed fresh herbs
  or parsley to garnish

Slice the mushrooms thinly and put in a salad bowl. Heat the oil and sauté the onion and garlic until soft but not browned. Cool and add to the mushrooms. Add all the other ingredients and mix well. When ready to serve, sprinkle with fresh herbs or parsley.

This salad is much improved if allowed to stand for a few hours. It will even keep well overnight in a refrigerator. Cover it to avoid flavours travelling.

Dried Fruit Compote

1 lb/450g dried fruit
10 fl oz/300ml water
4 fl oz/100ml red wine
Thinly peeled rind and juice of
  a large lemon
5 oz/150g caster sugar
1 teaspoon allspice

Make up a mixture of dried fruit selected from apples, apricots, pitted prunes, sultanas, pears, dates and figs. Soak the fruit as necessary. In a saucepan combine the water, wine, lemon rind and juice, sugar and allspice. Bring to the boil, stirring until the sugar dissolves. Boil for 5 minutes to form a syrup. Then add the soaked dried fruit and simmer for 20 to 30 minutes.

Good served hot or cold, alone or with a dollop of crème fraîche.

Summer Fruit Moulds

6 thick slices of milk loaf
1 lb/450 g fresh soft fruit
½ pint/250 ml water
Sugar to taste
2 tablespoons cassis or
  elderflower cordial
Extra fruit and sprigs of fresh
  mint or lemon balm to
  garnish

These quantities will fill six ramekins

For the fruit choose any combination of raspberries, blackcurrants, gooseberries, blackberries and strawberries; try to use at least two varieties. Cut the crusts off the bread and cut the slices into large dice. Put the fruit in a saucepan, cover with water and simmer until the fruit is tender. Gooseberries and blackcurrants need 5 minutes or so; strawberries, blackberries and raspberries just need to be brought up to the boil and then removed from the heat immediately. Remove the fruit from the juice with a slotted spoon and add sufficient sugar to the juice to make a syrup. This will vary according to fruits and taste. I use about 4 oz/125 g with a mixture of blackcurrants and loganberries. Bring the syrup to the boil and simmer for 5 minutes. Allow to cool and add the cassis or elderflower cordial. Mix the fruit and bread together. Put a little syrup in the bottom of each ramekin, then pack in the fruit and bread pressing the mixture down well. Spoon a little syrup over the top of each ramekin. Chill until required.

To serve run a knife round the inside of each ramekin and unmould on to a dessert plate. Pour over the rest of the juice and decorate with more fresh fruit and sprigs of fresh mint or lemon balm.

Cornish Fairings

4 oz/125 g butter or margarine
4 oz/125 g caster sugar
4 fl oz/100 ml syrup
8 oz/225 g plain flour sifted with:
2 level teaspoons each of baking
  powder, bicarbonate of soda,
  ground ginger
1 level teaspoon mixed spice

Preheat oven to 150°C, 300°F, gas mark 2. Cream the butter, sugar and syrup together until well mixed, light and fluffy. Add the flour and spices so that you have a soft dough. Make the dough into balls about the size of a walnut and put on a tray either well greased and floured or lined with baking paper. Flatten each ball slightly and keep them well apart. Bake approx. 15 minutes. Cool on a wire tray.

Fairings are thin, crisp, spicy biscuits, approx. 3 to 4 in/ 8 to 10 cm in diameter with a characteristic cracked surface.

WALLINGTON
NORTHUMBERLAND

Drive north-east across the bleak, beautiful Northumbrian moors from Newcastle and suddenly, over the brow of a hill, Wallington appears below, a grey Palladian mansion approached over a handsome bridge and guarded by four huge stone griffins' heads.

Since 1688 Wallington has belonged to two families, the Blacketts and the Trevelyans. Both had a tradition of public service and both produced men and women of energy, intelligence and individuality.

In the 1760s Walter Calverley Blackett remodelled the house, built the elegant stable block and created the beautiful walled garden reached through woods below the house. This energetic man transformed the estate, was mayor of Newcastle five times and sat as an MP at Westminster in seven parliaments. He was called 'the Patriot' or 'The Opposer of the Court' at Westminster. Two magnificent Bristol Delft punch bowls commemorating his election in 1741 are still in the entrance hall. 'He had most of the virtues that cause a man to be beloved, and a large assortment of frailties which, in those far from Puritanical days, told rather for than against his personal popularity.' This slightly barbed anonymous comment may refer to his reputation for flirting with local ladies.

'Let us drink success to Blackett ...' is inscribed on one of the bowls. A century later Walter and Pauline Trevelyan, both fervent members of the temperance movement, would have insisted that the punch was non-alcoholic. Despite this they were certainly not puritans. He was interested in botany, geology, antiquities and agriculture. Pauline was clever, well-educated for a Victorian girl and artistic. Walter was much older than her and he allowed her to cultivate friendships with writers, poets and artists who interested her. John Ruskin was a great friend, so was the poet Swinburne and the Pre-Raphaelite painter Holman Hunt. Ruskin and Pauline both planned and helped William Bell Scott to paint the murals which decorate the central hall at Wallington.

Staying with Walter and Pauline must have been stimulating but perhaps not comfortable. The diarist Augustus Hare grumbled that 'the house is like a great desert with one or two oases' and that lunch 'was as peculiar as everything else (Lady Trevelyan and her artists feeding solely on artichokes and cauliflowers)'. Yet even he enjoyed himself 'Everything either of them says is worth hearing and they are so full of information of every kind, that the time here has been all too short. . . .'

Today, time for the visitor at Wallington still seems 'all too short'. Do leave enough time though, not only to tour the house, but also to walk through the woods to the exquisite terraced garden which forms a sheltered haven in the wild Northumbrian landscape. Finally visit the Clocktower Restaurant in the stables. Northern housewives traditionally pride themselves on their preserves. I am particularly pleased to have a delicious Victorian chutney recipe.

Pumpkin and Tomato Soup

3 tablespoons olive oil
8 oz/225 g onion, finely chopped
3 sticks celery, finely chopped
2 lb/900 g pumpkin, peeled and
   cut in chunks
1 lb/450 g tomatoes, peeled and
   chopped
2½ pints/1.5 litres vegetable
   stock
2 tablespoons tomato paste
Dried thyme
Salt and pepper to taste
Chopped parsley to garnish

Heat the oil and sauté the onion and celery until soft but not coloured. Add the pumpkin and tomatoes and turn them in the oil for a couple of minutes. Add the stock, tomato paste, and dried thyme to taste – I used about half a teaspoon. Simmer for approx. 40 minutes. Blend until smooth, season to taste with salt and pepper and serve very hot garnished with chopped parsley.

These quantities make at least 8 to 10 portions of soup, but since it is difficult to buy pumpkin in small quantities, I have not reduced them. The soup freezes well, should there be leftovers.

Beef and Ham Terrine

12 oz/350 g best minced beef
12 oz/350 g minced cooked ham
2 oz/50 g fresh breadcrumbs
1 teaspoon mixed herbs
½ teaspoon sage
2 eggs, beaten
Salt and pepper to taste

Preheat oven to 180°C, 350°F, gas mark 4. Grease a loaf tin large enough to take all the ingredients, approx. 1½ lb/ 675 g. Put all the ingredients except the eggs in a large bowl and mix together evenly. Stir in the eggs and transfer the mixture to the loaf tin, pressing it in well and smoothing the top. Cover with a layer of greaseproof paper and layer of foil and stand the loaf tin in a roasting tin. Fill the roasting tin with water to come half way up the loaf tin. Bake one hour. Allow to cool and chill overnight. Unmould on to a serving dish and serve cold. Red Cabbage Pickle (p.145) or Frances's Spicy Apple and Onion Chutney (p.144) are good accompanying relishes.

Chestnut, Mushroom and Cranberry Lattice Pie

12oz/350g shortcrust pastry
Egg wash

FILLING
1 tablespoon sunflower oil
1 small onion, peeled and
    chopped
1 clove garlic, crushed
4oz/125g rice (long grain or
    arborio)
Pinch of thyme
¾ pint/400ml vegetable stock
4oz/125g chestnuts, peeled
2oz/50g cranberries
1oz/25g pistachio nuts,
    dehusked
4oz/125g mushrooms
    (if possible mixed) chopped
    into chunks

GLAZE
1 tablespoon water
2oz/50g cranberry sauce
1 dessertspoon wine vinegar
2oz/50g cranberries

Preheat oven to 180°C, 350°F, gas mark 4. Roll out the pastry and use three-quarters to line a 9in/23cm flan dish. Prick the base and bake 15 minutes to part cook the case. Melt the oil and sauté the onion and garlic until soft but not coloured. Stir in thyme and rice and add vegetable stock. Cover, bring to the boil, reduce the heat and simmer for approx. 25 minutes. Cool slightly, add chestnuts, cranberries, pistachio nuts and mushrooms. Fill the part-cooked pastry case with the mixture. Roll out the remaining pastry and use to make a lattice topping. Brush with egg wash and return to the oven for a further 30 minutes.

Make up the glaze by putting all the ingredients except the cranberries in a small pan and boiling until the mixture is reduced by half. Stir in the cranberries, cook for a minute or two until they begin to 'pop', then spoon over the top of the pie.

Wallington's Christmas solution for non-turkey eaters: seasonal, nutty and lovely to look at.

Frances's Spicy Apple and Onion Chutney

3lb/1350g apples, peeled, cored
    and chopped
2lb/900g onion, sliced finely
1½lb/675g raisins
2oz/50g yellow mustard seeds
2 pints/1250ml malt vinegar
8oz/225g chopped fresh
    tomatoes
4 teaspoons salt
8oz/225g caster sugar
2 teaspoons Cayenne pepper

Put all the ingredients in a preserving pan and bring to the boil, stirring while the sugar dissolves. Boil all together for an hour. Pot and cover when cold. Makes 10 jars.

Don't worry if it seems a little liquid at first; it thickens as it matures.

Red Cabbage Pickle

3lb/1350g red cabbage
1 onion
About 1 tablespoon salt
2 dessertspoons soft brown
    sugar
1½ pints/750ml cider or wine
    vinegar
8oz/225g caster sugar
½ teaspoon mixed spice
6 peppercorns
1 teaspoon whole cloves
2 cinnamon sticks

Slice the cabbage and the onion finely and mix with salt in a large bowl. Put all the rest of the ingredients in a saucepan and bring to the boil, stirring while the sugar dissolves. Transfer to a china or plastic container and leave both to stand overnight.

Next day, put the cabbage and onion into jars, packing it as tightly as you can. Pour over the vinegar mixture and leave it at least three days before using as a relish. It will keep for several months. It is a traditional accompaniment to Lancashire Hot Pot and is delicious with the Irish Stew recipe on p.66. At Wallington it is served with the Ham and Beef Terrine.

Vegetarian Christmas Pudding

8oz/225g raisins
6oz/175g sultanas
6oz/175g currants
2oz/50g candied peel
1oz/25g flaked almonds
1oz/25g flour
1 teaspoon mixed spice
1 teaspoon cinnamon
½ teaspoon nutmeg
4oz/125g caster sugar
4oz/125g fresh white
    breadcrumbs
Grated rind and juice of
    1 lemon
1oz/25g butter or margarine
2 eggs
¼ pint/150ml orange juice

In a large bowl mix together the raisins, sultanas, currants, candied peel and almonds. Sieve the flour with the mixed spice, cinnamon and nutmeg. Add to the fruit, together with sugar and breadcrumbs, grated rind and juice of lemon, and the diced butter. Mix thoroughly. Beat the eggs well with the orange juice and stir into the mixture. Leave to stand overnight. The next day, pack into pudding basins. There is probably sufficient mixture for one large and one small or two medium-sized basins. Leave at least an inch/2.5cm at the top for expansion. Cover with greaseproof paper and foil and tuck it down round the rim. Stand the basins on top of upturned saucers in a saucepan. Fill the saucepan with water to halfway up the basins and simmer for at least 3 hours.

The puddings will then keep for as many months as you want. They taste just as good even a year later. On Christmas Day, re-cover with fresh paper and foil and steam for an hour before serving.

This mixture is particularly light and lemony, a great favourite with Wallington visitors.

Cheese and Herb Scones

1lb/450g self-raising flour
2 teaspoons mixed herbs
1 teaspoon baking powder
2oz/50g baking margarine
8oz/225g red Leicester cheese
2oz/50g Parmesan cheese
1 egg mixed with a little milk

Preheat oven to 230°C, 450°F, gas mark 8. Grease a baking sheet or line it with baking paper. Sift the flour with the herbs and baking powder. Rub the margarine into the flour. Grate the cheeses finely. Retaining a little of the red Leicester, add the rest to the mixture, together with the Parmesan. Use the egg and milk to form a soft dough. Knead this very lightly, then turn it out on to a floured surface and roll or pat out to 1 in/2.5 cm thickness. Cut into 2 in/5 cm rounds and place on the prepared baking sheet. Brush the tops with a little milk and scatter a little grated cheese on each. Bake approx. 10 minutes, until well risen and golden brown. Cool on a wire rack.

Traditionally scones in Northumberland are served with soup. There is a recipe for Leek and Onion Scones from Souter Lighthouse, another property in the north-east, on p.121.

Apple Cheesecake

BASE
2oz/50g butter
2oz/50g sugar
4oz/125g crushed digestive
   biscuits

FILLING
2 eggs
4oz/125g caster sugar
8oz/225g full-fat cream cheese
1 teaspoon cinnamon
¼ pint/150ml apple purée
2oz/50g sultanas
¼ pint/150ml crème fraîche
¼ pint/150ml creamy milk

TOPPING
Fresh apple slices dipped in
   lemon juice
Whipped cream

Preheat oven to 180°C, 350°F, gas mark 4. Melt the butter and sugar, stir in the biscuit crumbs and press into the base of a 9in/23cm oiled springform tin.

Beat the eggs with the sugar until thick and creamy. Then gradually beat in the cream cheese. Stir in cinnamon, apple purée, sultanas, crème fraîche and milk. Pour the mixture into the tin and cook for approx. 1 hour. The top should be firm but spongy to the touch. Turn off the oven, but leave the cheesecake in the oven to cool for another hour with the door open. Then chill until required. To serve, run a knife round the inside of the tin to release the cheesecake, place it on a serving dish and decorate with apple slices and rosettes of whipped cream.

WATERSMEET
DEVON

'The spot was made by nature for herself . . .'. If you look carefully you will still see this quotation from Wordsworth carved in 1832 into the lintel over the front door of the Reverend Walter Stephen Halliday's delightful fishing lodge at Watersmeet.

Watersmeet is a spectacularly beautiful valley where the rivers East Lyn and Hoar Oak meet. The National Trust now owns 340 acres of land here. There are signed long walks for serious ramblers as well as less strenuous paths winding down the steep hillsides to where the water tumbles over mossy boulders.

Poet, fisherman, eccentric and joker, the Reverend Halliday was determined to live as a true Romantic. He divided his time between Switzerland and Devon, drinking in the picturesque scenery and entertaining other artistic friends. For forty years he fished, entertained and wrote poems here and bought as much of the beautiful valleys as he could lay his hands on.

Small wooden bridges lead to the green and white painted lodge. A consciously rustic note is the untrimmed tree trunks which form the uprights of the otherwise formally elegant verandah. I think these might be Halliday's way of poking gentle fun at the excesses of the Romantic movement. Today's walkers may still be fooled by him if they discover a Roman coin during their ramble. The Romans were not here first, Halliday was. One of his hobbies was to go on excursions with a pocket full of old coins, scattering and burying them in places where gullible archaeologists might find them.

After his death the house was leased to the Necombe family, bakers and confectioners. They began serving teas in 1901, a delicious tradition which continues to this day. Nothing can beat the pleasure of listening to the rush of the water, watching the play of sunlight through the leaves of the trees while demolishing one of the wonderful cakes on offer. For that experience you must visit Watersmeet, but here are recipes for a luscious Mincemeat Slice and a splendid Vegetarian Lasagne.

Mincemeat Slice

8 oz/225 g self-raising flour
4 oz/125 g chilled butter or
margarine
4 oz/125 g caster sugar
1 egg, beaten
8 oz/225 g mincemeat
2 eating apples
Milk and demerara sugar to
finish

Preheat oven to 180°C, 350°F, gas mark 4. Rub the fat into the flour until the mixture resembles coarse breadcrumbs. Stir in the caster sugar and beaten egg and work the mixture into a smooth dough. Chill for at least 30 minutes.

Grease an 8 in × 14 in/23 cm × 33 cm Swiss roll tin or line it with baking paper. Divide the dough in two. Roll each half out to fit the tin with enough overlap to allow you to seal the slice when it is filled. Lay the first half in the tin and cover with mincemeat, spreading it evenly. Peel and slice the apples thinly and lay on top of the mincemeat. Roll out the rest of the pastry, cover the fruit completely and seal the edges with milk. Brush with milk and sprinkle with demerara sugar. Bake for 30 to 40 minutes, until crisp and golden. Cut into squares and serve warm with ice-cream, crème fraîche or cream.

At Watersmeet, Mincemeat Slice is served with thick golden Devon clotted cream – a real treat after a good walk.

Vegetarian Lasagne

1 medium aubergine, chopped
2 × 14oz/400g tins of chopped tomatoes*
2 tablespoons tomato purée*
1 dessertspoon mixed herbs*
1 teaspoon sugar*
Salt and pepper to taste*
3oz/75g butter*
3oz/75g flour*
1½ pints/750ml creamy milk*
6oz/175g Cheddar cheese, grated*
1 packet ready cook lasagne*
Approx. 4 tablespoons vegetable oil*
1 large onion, peeled and chopped*
3 sticks celery, chopped
2 large carrots, peeled and cut into thin sticks
1 green pepper, de-seeded and cut into chunks
1 red pepper, de-seeded and cut into chunks
2 leeks, washed and chopped
2 courgettes, peeled and chopped
4oz/125g button mushrooms, halved
4oz/125g sweetcorn

Do not worry if you have not got all the vegetables listed; use fewer varieties and put in more of each. The essential ingredients are asterisked.

Preheat oven to 180°C, 350°F, gas mark 4. Salt the aubergine and leave to stand at least 30 minutes to get rid of any bitterness. Mix the chopped tomatoes, tomato purée, mixed herbs and sugar together and add salt and pepper to taste. Make a cheese sauce using the butter, flour, milk and 3oz/75g of the grated Cheddar. You are now ready to start assembling the lasagne. Dot a little of the tomato mixture on the bottom of a roasting tin or large ovenproof dish. Cover this with single sheets of lasagne (break them to make them fit if you have to). Melt a couple of spoons of oil in a frying-pan and sauté each of the vegetables for 5 minutes or so. Lift them out with a slotted spoon and spread over the lasagne. Salt and pepper as you go. Use the rest of the oil to top up in the frying-pan if you need to. When the lasagne is completely covered, dot the vegetables with tomato sauce and cover them with a second layer of lasagne sheets. Rinse and dry the aubergine chunks before frying them. Finish with mushrooms and sweetcorn which do not need sautéing. Dot with the rest of the tomato. Cover with a third layer of lasagne sheets and spread the cheese sauce over them. Finish with a layer of grated cheese. Bake for an hour. The lasagne should then be cooked and the top crisp and golden.

This is a magnificent recipe for any hungry crowd and I have not reduced it. It does take time to make but it is a complete meal in one dish and preparation can be done well in advance. All it needs is good bread to mop up the juice.

YORK TEA-ROOM

The Great Hall, Treasurer's House, York

Profits from National Trust city shops and restaurants, like those from the shops and restaurants at the properties, support the work of the National Trust.

Dominated by its magnificent Minster, York is a unique walled city full of history just waiting to be explored. The streets are thronged with locals and tourists of all nationalities, visiting the sites, shopping and enjoying York's special atmosphere.

The National Trust Tea-Room in York is just round the corner from the Treasurer's House, a fascinating Trust property, beautifully situated in the shadow of York Minster. Well worth a visit, it even helps York live up to its reputation as 'the most haunted city in Britain'. In 1960 Harry Martindale saw a whole Roman legion of ghosts while working in the cellars. A sad, dispirited and grubby group they looked, he said, but York must have been an unpopular posting for a Roman, cold, wet, harassed by hostile tribes and far from home.

Number 30 Goodramgate is light, modern, warm and inviting. All day and everyday except Sunday it serves food, using local specialities like Theakstons Ale to spice up old favourites. Locally grown vegetables feature in original soups and casseroles. Here too are two irresistible hot puddings which instantly put new life into tired tourists.

Cauliflower and Almond Soup

3oz/75g butter
1 medium onion, chopped
1 medium cauliflower, divided
   into florets
4oz/125g flaked almonds
¼ teaspoon nutmeg
¼ teaspoon turmeric
1½ pints/750ml vegetable stock
Salt and pepper to taste

Melt the butter in a large saucepan. Sauté the onion until soft but not coloured, then add the cauliflower, almonds, nutmeg and turmeric. Stir well so that all ingredients are thoroughly combined and cook gently for 5 minutes. Add the vegetable stock, bring to the boil, then reduce the heat and simmer until the cauliflower is cooked. Blend the soup until it is smooth, season with salt and pepper to taste. Reheat if necessary and serve with a scatter of toasted almonds on the top.

Leek and Lemon Soup

1lb/450g leeks
2oz/50g butter
1 tablespoon wholemeal flour
2 teaspoons mustard powder
1½ pints/750ml vegetable stock
Juice and grated rind of 1 lemon
1 tablespoon chopped parsley
Swirl of cream to serve

Chop the leeks finely. Melt the butter in a large saucepan and sauté the leeks for approx. 10 minutes, until soft but not brown. Then stir in the flour and mustard. Cool the mixture for a minute or two and add the stock, stirring well. Bring to the boil, add the lemon rind and simmer for 15 minutes with the lid off. Just before serving, add the lemon juice and parsley. Add a swirl of cream to each soup bowl and serve immediately.

Tart and interesting – a connoisseur's soup!

Haddock and Prawn Cobbler

1½ lb/675 g haddock fillet,
   skinned and cut into 2 in/5 cm
   chunks
2 oz/50 g butter
2 oz/50 g plain flour
2 teaspoons dry mustard
1 pint/500 ml milk
2 dessertspoons wine vinegar
2 hardboiled eggs, peeled and
   chopped
2 oz/50 g prawns

TOPPING
6 oz/175 g wholemeal flour
1 tablespoon baking powder
Pinch thyme
1½ oz/40 g butter
1 egg, beaten
2 tablespoons milk

Preheat oven to 180°C, 350°F, gas mark 4. Cook haddock in boiling water. This will take approx. 10 minutes. Allow to cool. Make a white sauce with the butter, flour and mustard powder, using the milk and wine vinegar as liquid. Don't worry if the sauce curdles; just give it a quick whisk. Lay the cooked haddock in an 8 in × 9 in/20 cm × 23 cm china gratin dish, approx. 2.5 in/6.5 cm deep. Sprinkle over the prawns and chopped hardboiled eggs and cover with white sauce. Put aside while you make the topping.

Sift together flour, baking powder and thyme into a large bowl. Rub in the butter, then make up into a dough using the egg and milk. Roll out into a sheet approx. 1 in/2.5 cm thick and cut into 2 in/5 cm rounds. Arrange on the top of the fish mixture. Brush with milk and bake for approx. 20 minutes, until well risen and brown. Serve with green vegetables or a green salad.

Mushroom, Nut and Tomato Savoury Bake

6 fl oz/175 ml vegetable oil
1 lb/450 g fresh breadcrumbs
8 oz/225 g walnut pieces
1 medium onion, chopped
1 lb/450 g button mushrooms,
   chopped
1 lb/450 g fresh tomatoes,
   chopped
A handful of chopped basil
Pepper and salt to taste

Preheat oven to 190°C, 375°F, gas mark 5. Heat half the oil and fry the breadcrumbs, nuts and onion for 5 minutes. Set the pan aside. In a separate pan fry the mushrooms for 2 minutes, add the chopped tomatoes, basil and season to taste. Cook for a further 5 minutes.

In a shallow gratin dish spread a layer of half the crumbs, top with a layer of mushrooms and tomatoes and finish with the rest of the crumbs. Bake for 30 minutes, until brown and crunchy.

Theakston's Old Peculier Beef Casserole

1 tablespoon sunflower oil
Either all or a selection of the
  following vegetables:
1 medium onion, sliced
2 medium carrots, peeled and
  sliced
8 oz/225 g swede, peeled and
  chopped
1 medium parsnip, peeled and
  chopped
1 lb/450 g braising steak cut into
  large chunks
2 tablespoons plain flour mixed
  with pepper and salt to taste
1 teaspoon mixed herbs
  (optional)
Large can Theakston's Old
  Peculier bitter

Preheat oven to 140°C, 275°F, gas mark 1. Heat the oil and gently sauté the vegetables for approx. 10 minutes. Remove with a slotted spoon and put in a cast-iron casserole. Toss the meat in the seasoned flour and brown well in the remaining oil, adding a little more oil if necessary. Add to the vegetables. Heat the beer gently and pour over the meat and vegetables. Bring the casserole to the boil, then place in the oven and cook for 2 to 3 hours, or until the meat is tender. Adjust seasoning if necessary.

Serve with a Yorkshire pudding (below), and a glass of Theakston's for an authentic combination of flavours.

Yorkshire Pudding

6 oz/175 g plain flour
2 eggs, well beaten
Water to mix
½ pint/250 ml milk
Salt and pepper to taste
Approx. 1 oz/25 g hard fat,
  such as Trex

In a mixing bowl stir the eggs into the flour and add sufficient water to make a smooth paste. Beat in the milk until the consistency of the mix is similar to unwhipped double cream. Leave to stand for 30 minutes.

Preheat oven to 220°C, 450°F, gas mark 7. Ideally you should use an 8 in × 6 in/20 cm × 16 cm oblong tin, though individual pudding tins may be more practical. Put a knob of fat in the tin or tins and heat in the oven until the fat smokes. Divide the mixture among the tins and bake for 15 minutes, until risen and golden brown. If cooking 1 large pudding this will probably require an extra 5 minutes.

Essentials for a good Yorkshire Pudding are very hot fat, not too much of it and a good hot oven. If you are serving this with Theakston's Old Peculier Beef Casserole, I suggest you let the casserole rest in a warm place for the 20 minutes the puddings take to cook. The casserole will remain hot enough, and the meat should be meltingly tender.

Root Vegetables in Turmeric and Coconut Sauce

1¼ pint/650 ml milk
6 oz/175 g desiccated coconut
3 tablespoons vegetable oil
1 large onion, sliced
2 cloves garlic, chopped fine
2 teaspoons grated fresh ginger
2 teaspoons turmeric
12 oz/350 g each of carrots,
    swede and parsnip, peeled
    and cut into chunks
1 green pepper, de-seeded and
    chopped fine
Salt and pepper to taste
Coriander or parsley to garnish

Heat milk to boiling point and pour over the coconut. Cover and leave to infuse while preparing the vegetables. Heat the oil and fry the onion until soft but not browned. Stir in the garlic, ginger and turmeric and cook a further 2 to 3 minutes. Add the chopped carrots, swede and parsnip. Turn well in the mixture. Then strain the milk over them. Press the coconut well in the sieve to extract all flavour and add one-third to the mixture. Add the green pepper, season to taste with salt and pepper. Cover the pan and simmer the mixture gently for 15 to 20 minutes, until the vegetables are cooked but not mushy. If you think the sauce is too thin, cream a little of the liquid with a level dessertspoon of cornflour and return to the pan to thicken it. Serve with rice garnished with chopped fresh coriander or parsley.

Mushroom and Lentil Burgers

1 oz/25 g butter
1 tablespoon vegetable oil
1 medium onion, chopped fine
1 lb/450 g mushrooms, chopped
2 cloves garlic
4 oz/125 g red lentils
2 tablespoons parsley, chopped
    fine
Salt and pepper to taste
Flour for coating
Oil for frying

If you intend to bake the burgers, preheat oven to 200°C, 400°F, gas mark 6. Heat the butter and oil in a large pan. Fry the chopped onion for 5 minutes, then add the chopped mushrooms and garlic. Stir and fry gently on a moderate heat until all the liquid has evaporated and the mixture resembles a thick purée. Take the pan off the heat and leave to cool while you cook the lentils. Put the lentils in a saucepan, just cover with water, bring to the boil, then reduce the heat and simmer until tender. Drain off surplus water if necessary. Cool the lentils until lukewarm – they should thicken up – then mix in the mushroom mixture, parsley and salt and pepper to taste. Form the mixture into burgers; it should make 4 to 6. Roll the burgers in flour and fry quickly in a little hot oil or bake for approx. 30 minutes. Serve with the Spicy Tomato Sauce on p.14.

Treacle Sponge Pudding

8 oz/225 g butter
8 oz/225 g soft brown sugar
4 eggs
12 oz/350 g self-raising flour
1 teaspoon vanilla essence
½ pint/250 ml golden syrup
¼ pint/150 ml water

Preheat oven to 180°C, 350°F, gas mark 4. Cream butter and sugar until light and fluffy. Beat in eggs, adding a spoonful of flour with each egg. Stir in vanilla essence and fold in the rest of the flour. Grease a white china dish, approx. 8 in × 9 in/20 cm × 23 cm, put in the mixture, smoothing the top. Bake until golden brown and firm to the touch, approx. 30 to 35 minutes.

Heat the syrup and water in the microwave until blended, or stir together in a small saucepan. Prick the top of the pudding with a skewer and pour over the treacle mixture so that the pudding is evenly covered.

Serve warm, accompanied by the custard recipe on p.27.

Chocolate Fudge Pudding

4 oz/125 g butter
4 oz/125 g caster sugar
2 eggs
6 oz/175 g self-raising flour
2 level tablespoons cocoa
A little milk if necessary

½ pint/250 ml water
3 oz/75 g brown sugar
3 level tablespoons cocoa

Preheat oven to 180°C, 350°F, gas mark 4. Butter an oven-proof dish, approx. 3 in/10 cm deep and 8 in × 9 in/20 cm × 23 cm in diameter. Cream the butter and sugar until pale and fluffy. Beat in the eggs, adding one spoon of the flour with each egg. Fold in the flour and cocoa, sifted together. If the mixture seems too stiff, fold in a little milk until it is a suitable mixture to spread in the dish.

Gently heat the water, sugar and cocoa in a saucepan until the sugar is dissolved and the mixture resembles a thinnish sauce. Pour the sauce over the pudding mixture and bake for 45 minutes to 1 hour, until the top is crisp and brown.

Serve warm. The pudding will have risen through the sauce, combining a rich dark moist base with a crisp top. For total indulgence serve with extra pouring cream.

US CONVERSION TABLE

Information very kindly provided by the Good Housekeeping Institute

DRY MEASURES

1 US cup	=	50 g	=	2 oz of:	breadcrumbs; fresh cake crumbs
1 US cup	=	75 g	=	3 oz of:	rolled oats
1 US cup	=	90 g	=	3½ oz of:	desiccated coconut; ground almonds
1 US cup	=	100 g	=	4 oz of:	suet; grated hard cheese; walnut pieces; drinking chocolate; icing sugar; cocoa; flaked almonds; pasta; frozen peas
1 US cup	=	125 g	=	5 oz of:	white flour; self-raising flour; currants; muesli; chopped dates; ground roasted almonds
1 US cup	=	150 g	=	5½ oz of:	wholemeal flour; raisins; cornflour
1 US cup	=	175 g	=	6 oz of:	apricots; mixed peel; sultanas
1 US cup	=	200 g	=	7 oz of:	caster sugar; soft brown sugar; demerara sugar; glacé cheries; lentils; long grain and brown rice; flaked and drained tuna fish
1 US cup	=	225 g	=	½ oz of:	cream cheese; cottage cheese
1 US cup	=	300 g	=	11 oz of:	mincemeat; marmalade
1 US cup	=	350 g	=	12 oz of:	syrup; treacle; jam

LIQUID MEASURES

¼ US cup	=	60 ml	=	2 fluid oz
1 US cup	=	240 ml	=	8 fluid oz
2 US cups (1 US pint)	=	480 ml	=	16 fluid oz

BUTTER, LARD AND MARGARINE MEASURES

¼ stick	=	25 g	=	2 level tablespoons	=	1 oz
1 stick (½ US cup)	=	100 g	=	8 level tablespoons	=	4 oz

INDEX